A Celebrated Industry

The Historic Wares of Southeastern Massachusetts,
Bristol County and Cape Cod

Justin W. Thomas

Historic Beverly

Beverly, Massachusetts

Copyright © 2022 by **Justin W. Thomas**

All rights reserved. No part of this publication may be reproduced, distributed or transmitted in any form or by any means, without prior written permission.

Justin W. Thomas/Historic Beverly
117 Cabot Street
Beverly, Mass. 01915
Historicbeverly.net

A Celebrated Industry: The Historic Wares of Southeastern Massachusetts, Bristol County and Cape Cod/ Justin W. Thomas. -- 1st ed.

ISBN 978-1-891906-06-0

Dedicated to my niece, Alexis, nephew, Jason, my parents and my sister, Meghan.

"Tell me and I forget. Teach me and I remember. Involve me and I learn."

–BENJAMIN FRANKLIN

> Contents

Preface | 7

Introduction | 23

1. Eighteenth Century Red Earthenware Production in Abington and Quincy, Mass. | 40
2. The Wares Manufactured in Braintree, Mass. and Lyndeborough, New Hampshire | 60
3. The Bradford Family Pottery in Kingston, Mass. | 82
4. The Archaeology of the Kingston Pottery | 95
5. The Red Earthenware Industry in Bristol County, Mass. | 122
6. Elijiah Cornell's Pottery Production | 156
7. The Bradford Family Pottery in West Barnstable, Mass. on Cape Cod | 171
8. The Archaeology of the Barnstable Pottery | 181
9. The Historical Significance of the Potteries in Southeastern Massachusetts, Bristol County and Cape Cod | 203
10. Illustrations | 209
    a. Partially Glazed Household Wares | 210
    b. Animal Wares | 211
    c. Flowerpots | 212
    d. Marriage Jars & Other Significant Pieces | 213
    e. Glazed Household Wares | 220
11. List of Some of the Potters Employed in Southeastern Massachusetts, Bristol County and Cape Cod | 457

Appendix:
Bibliography | 465

> Preface

American red earthenware has been a brand of utilitarian pottery production sought after by collectors and museums for well over a century now. The Pennsylvania German sgraffito wares were some of the earliest styles in demand. Understandably, many of the best examples disappeared from the American marketplace when they were acquired by such figures as Edwin Atlee Barber (1851-1916) for the Philadelphia Museum of Art, as early as the late nineteenth century, and Winterthur Museum in Delaware by Henry Francis du Pont (1880-1869), beginning in the 1920s.

However, it was actually a New Englander who was amid the first wave of true collectors in America. According to the Wadsworth Atheneum Museum of Art in Hartford, Connecticut, "Albert Hastings Pitkin (1852-1917) was among the first to systematically study and collect early American pottery. While visiting a local farmhouse in the spring of 1884, his discovery of two pieces of redware, or lead glazed (red) earthenware pottery, spurred his passion for ceramics. Pitkin soon amassed a collection and became known as the leading authority on New England earthenware. In 1910 he joined the staff at the Wadsworth Atheneum as curator of the department of ceramics. During his tenure, he oversaw the installation of his own collections in the J. Pierpont Morgan Memorial collection of decorative arts, and upon his death, his wife, Sarah Howard Loomis Pitkin (1851-1921), donated over 300 objects to the museum."

This is Albert Hastings Pitkin (1852-1917). (courtesy Wadsworth Atheneum Museum of Art)

Although, it did not take long before other collectors emerged in New England, such as Charles D. Cook in Providence, Rhode Island and Cape Cod, and Massachusetts collectors Mr.

A Celebrated Industry

and Mrs. William Whitman Junior, as well as Massachusetts author Lura Woodside Watkins (1897-1982), who published the landmark book, *Early New England Potters and Their Wares* in 1950.

In spite of that, it apparently took some time for New England red earthenware to become a noticeable fixture within New England auction houses, even though local auctioneers had recognized wares from the Mid-Atlantic region decades prior.

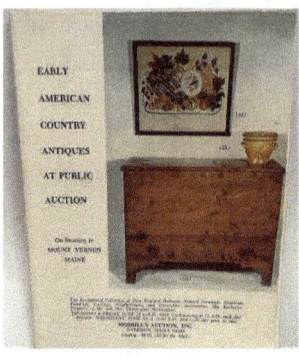

The Huntington Collection auction catalog.

Some may even say that the first major sale of New England red earthenware took place on Thursday June 20 and Friday June 21, 1974, at Morrill's Auction Company in Harrison, Maine, when the Mr. and Mrs. Christopher Huntington Collection of Americana was sold. The sale included many objects of red earthenware manufactured throughout New England, but there were also products made in Pennsylvania, which may have functioned as accent pieces in the Huntington's home.

Two red earthenware pitchers that sold in the Huntington Collection where their origin in New England has been questioned through the years.

The Huntington Collection was not exclusive to a single area, region, or state, like many people and institutions collect today. Instead, it seems that the Huntingtons were principally drawn to the aesthetics of pottery, and perhaps equally shared a love of the wares produced all over New England.

The Huntington Collection also contained a few colorful red earthenware pitchers; in one way or another, the origin of these pitchers has been a subject of debate ever since the sale. The refinement and skill seem to represent coastal Massachusetts production, whereas the colors used to create the glaze are loosely attributed to Maine's nineteenth century red earthenware industry. This is a subject that I have been fascinated with for some years now and have really made it an objective to try and determine what is the correct answer based on actual archaeological evidence, which will be discussed in this book. I will explain how these types of wares can be attributed to the Bradford family in Kingston, Massachusetts, based on archaeological evidence kept at the National Museum of American History at the Smithsonian Institute in Washington, D.C. and Plimouth Plantation in Plymouth, Massachusetts.

However, the red earthenware manufactured just to the south in Bristol County, Massachusetts in the eighteenth and nineteenth century has been desired for at least a century now by collectors, dealers, and museums. It is a combination of factors that have contributed to this infatuation, such as the refinement of the production, the color of the glazes and the history of the industry. The mere presence of just one of these objects can be romanticized today as a work of art, for which such an object was once partially viewed for its simple utilitarian purposes in the household, even though its colorful appearance was undoubtedly fashionable when it was originally produced.

The area's production first received widespread published recognition in the early-1930s with articles written for *The Magazine Antiques* by John Ramsay, as well as Charles D. Cook, whose collection descended in his family until it sold in multiple highly contested sales at Skinner in Boston in the early-2000s. The highlight of the collection was an incredible red earthenware jar dated *"1829,"* which featured a person's initials, *"A.P.B."* and a smaller jar as the finial on the lid. The elegance of

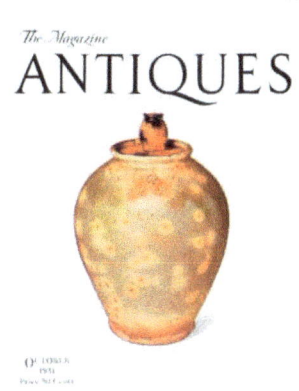

October 1931 issue of The Magazine Antiques with a Bristol County, Mass. presentation jar illustrated on the cover.

this jar graced the cover of the now famous October 1931 edition of *The Magazine Antiques*. After this jar sold at Skinner for $63,000, it went on to be featured at the Winter Antiques Show in New York City, where it now resides in an all-important private collection today.

These articles may have also helped inspire Henry Francis du Pont (1880-1969) with the collection he assembled at Winterthur in Delaware in the 1920s and 1930s, which features some objects that are very similar to what Cook published.

But even before this production was acknowledged in publication, it had been coveted by early twentieth century collectors like Cook, as well as the Whitmans, where some of their collection was featured in an American antiques exhibit in Park Square in Boston in 1925. This red earthenware must have influenced author John Spargo (1876-1966), who later featured some of the Whitmans collection when *Early American Pottery and China* was published in 1926.

Renowned New Hampshire antiques dealer Roger Bacon was even selling red earthenware to Old Sturbridge Village in Sturbridge, Massachusetts, as early as the 1950s, which included pottery made in southeastern Massachusetts. The objects he sold from Bristol County were primarily slip decorated dishes.

The first major antiques collection to feature red earthenware from this region at auction was likely the Huntington sale in Maine. The stunning glazed forms included lidded jars, pitchers,

Late eighteenth or early nineteenth century green glazed red earthenware jug attributed to Bristol County, Mass.

and harvest jugs, although, the Oliver E. Williams Collection from Rockport, Massachusetts that Richard Withington sold in July 1966 was also noteworthy.

More recently, though, longtime Falmouth, Massachusetts antiques dealers Hilary and Paulette Nolan's collection of red earthenware somewhat set precedent for how this industry is currently viewed today. Their collection had been assembled over roughly thirty years before it sold at Northeast Auctions in Manchester, New Hampshire in the summer of 2004. The context, history, and passion for which it took to assemble this once in a lifetime collection was marvelous, whereas many of the objects retained early histories of ownership from homeowners and dealers in southeastern Massachusetts, Bristol County, Cape Cod and Rhode Island.

The research for this book took several years to complete, such as studying various archaeology collections and reports, along with visiting museums and private collections across the country. I hope you enjoy reading it as much as I enjoyed researching the historic eighteenth and nineteenth century wares manufactured in southeastern Massachusetts, Bristol County and Cape Cod.

Justin W. Thomas
2022

Late eighteenth or early nineteenth century red earthenware jug attributed to Bristol County, Mass. (courtesy New York Historical Society)

A Celebrated Industry

Hilary & Paulette Nolan Collection.

Bristol County, Mass. harvest jugs from the Hilary & Paulette Nolan Collection. (courtesy Northeast Auctions)

Green glazed Bristol County, Mass. pottery from the Hilary & Paulette Nolan Collection. (courtesy Northeast Auctions)

A Celebrated Industry

Hilary & Paulette Nolan Collection.

Bristol County, Mass. jars from the Hilary & Paulette Nolan Collection, although the jar shown to the left in the front is from North Yarmouth, Maine. (courtesy Northeast Auctions)

Bristol County, Mass. pottery from the Hilary & Paulette Nolan Collection. (courtesy Northeast Auctions)

A Celebrated Industry

Ron & Penny Dionne Collection; a number of these pieces were manufactured in southeastern Mass. and Bristol County, Mass. (courtesy Ron & Penny Dionne and David Wheatcroft)

A Celebrated Industry

Some Bristol County, Mass. red earthenware mixed in with other New England pottery at the Colonel John Ashley House in Sheffield, Massachusetts.

Pair of red earthenware whale oil lamps probably from Bristol County, Mass. that are shown later in the book compared to a glass pair of lamps from either the New England Glass Co. or the Boston & Sandwich Glass Co. (courtesy Crocker Farm and the Corning Museum of Glass)

Green glazed lidded red earthenware jar possibly made in Bristol County, Mass. that sold in the Mr. and Mrs Christopher Huntington Sale in Maine in 1974. It was pictured twice in the auction catalog.

A Celebrated Industry

Some of the red earthenware from the Nina Fletcher Little (1903-1993) Collection at Cogswell's Grant in Essex, Mass., which includes pottery made in Bristol County, Mass. (courtesy Historic New England)

Late eighteenth or early nineteenth century green glazed red earthenware jug attributed to Bristol County, Mass. (courtesy Bruneau & Company)

16

A Celebrated Industry

Red earthenware owned by Sam Forsythe in Ohio – various examples of pottery from Bristol County, Mass. are illustrated. Some of these pieces are also shown elsewhere in this book. (courtesy Sam Forsythe)

A Celebrated Industry

Top and Bottom - Some examples of southeastern Mass. and Bristol County pottery included in Roger Pheulpin's collection. Some of these pieces are also shown elsewhere in this book. (courtesy Roger Pheulpin)

A Celebrated Industry

Some examples of southeastern Mass. and Bristol County pottery included in Roger Pheulpin's collection. Some of these pieces are also shown elsewhere in this book. (courtesy Roger Pheulpin)

Some examples of southeastern Mass. and Bristol County pottery included in Roger Pheulpin's collection; most of the jugs in the graduated set are either from Essex County, Mass. or Bristol County, Mass. (courtesy Roger Pheulpin)

A Celebrated Industry

Top and Bottom - Some examples of southeastern Mass. and Bristol County pottery that were once a part of Lewis Scranton's collection. Some of these pieces are also shown elsewhere in this book. (courtesy Lewis Scranton)

A Celebrated Industry

Various late eighteenth and early nineteenth century red earthenware pieces grouped with various other types of pottery. Some of the objects were previously owned by Hilary and Paulette Nolan. (courtesy Antiques & the Arts Weekly and a private collection)

Some late eighteenth and early nineteenth century red earthenware from Bristol County, Mass., among wares by other manufacturers. (courtesy Stephen-Douglas Antiques)

Nineteenth century red earthenware pitcher possibly manufactured in Massachusetts adorned with circa 1870s-1880s decoupage decoration. During that period, ladies of the middle and upper classes threw themselves into the trend of decoupage known as "Decalcomania." Crafters would apply paper images onto all sorts of objects, such as furniture, stoneware, and glassware. The paper could be pasted either on the interior or exterior of the object; when the paper was glued on the exterior, a thin varnish was applied to protect the designs. (courtesy Fall River Historical Society)

Three pieces of eighteenth or early nineteenth century slip decorated red earthenware from Bristol County, Mass. displayed in the James Mitchell Varnum (1748-1779) House Museum in East Greenwich, Rhode Island. (courtesy Varnum House Museum)

> Introduction

The area known as southeastern Massachusetts incorporates portions of Massachusetts located along Buzzards Bay, including the city of New Bedford and its suburbs. Despite the location of Cape Cod, which is the southernmost part of the state (excluding the islands), it is sometimes considered a location in itself. At its broadest definition, southeastern Massachusetts includes all of Plymouth and Bristol Counties, most of the cities and towns in Norfolk County and even some towns in Worcester County.

Prior to 1685, there were two separate colonies within the boundaries of present-day Massachusetts; the area around Plymouth and Cape Cod settled by the Pilgrims was known as Plymouth colony, or the Old Colony. By the mid-1640s its population numbered about 3,000 people. Although, the Old Colony was rapidly overshadowed by its Puritan neighbor to the north, the Massachusetts Bay Colony.

The history of southeastern Massachusetts, Bristol County and Cape Cod is rich, and its eighteenth and nineteenth century red earthenware production is just as much celebrated. Aesthetically speaking, this area's red earthenware production is some of the most visually attractive wares manufactured anywhere in America. The forms were refined, such as teardrop shaped jugs and jars that were reminiscent of similar formed porcelain ginger jars manufactured in China for centuries. Although ideally, it is the glazes that are so attractive today, and in some cases, these glazes can easily be viewed as works of art, displayed at any major art museum in America.

The most attractive of all these glazes are likely the greens that are known in a variety of shades today manufactured throughout this region; however, it is the bright vibrant colored greens that are the most attractive, such as some that are an emerald green. The Bristol County glazes are also often thinly applied and evenly spread, but the greens are typically a thicker glaze. And in some cases, the Bristol County potters also

A Celebrated Industry

mastered the technique to incorporate other glaze colors that were used with the green glaze. But it should not be mistaken that this was the only location in New England manufacturing this type of green glaze. In fact, there are similarities found with green glazes produced at the Dodge Pottery in Portland, Maine, the industry in North Yarmouth, Maine, as well as in Essex County, Massachusetts, other areas in New England, and even elsewhere, such as the John Bell (1800-1880) Pottery in Waynesboro, Pennsylvania and the William Eby (1831-1910) Pottery in Ontario, Canada.

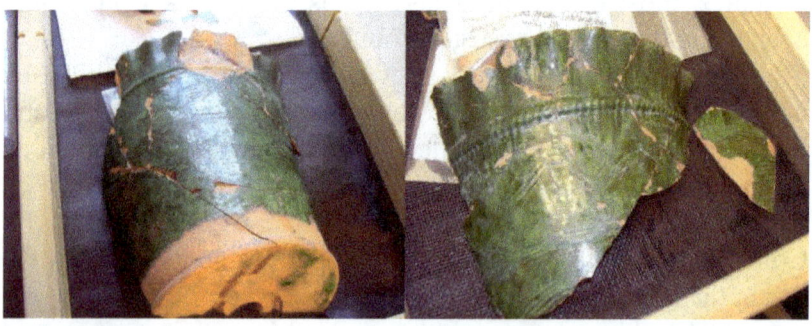

Nineteenth century green glazed red earthenware flowerpot recovered in Portsmouth, New Hampshire. (courtesy Strawbery Banke Archaeology Department)

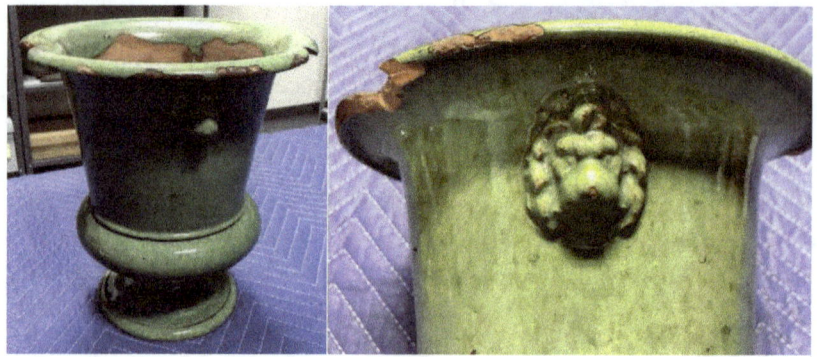

Two-piece nineteenth century green glazed red earthenware flowerpot adorned with two lion's heads made at the Dodge Pottery in Portland, Maine. (courtesy Maine Historical Society)

A Celebrated Industry

(Left) Red earthenware manufactured at the Eby Pottery in Ontario (Right) Green glazed red earthenware sherds recovered in North Yarmouth, Maine. (courtesy Canadian Museum of History & Yarmouth, Maine Historical Society)

Nineteenth century green glazed red earthenware flowerpot stamped "John Bell / Waynesboro."

Circa 1890-1910 green glazed red earthenware vase made by Emanuel Duschek in Chicago and possibly glazed by his wife Mary Duschek.

Nineteenth century green glazed red earthenware pitcher and bowl possibly made in coastal Massachusetts, although both were found in Yarmouth, Maine. (courtesy Sam Herrup)

Archaeological evidence has proven that wares from this region were shipped as far north as Boston and probably Charlestown, Massachusetts, and all over the southern part of coastal Massachusetts, Cape Cod, Nantucket and probably

Martha's Vineyard. But Rhode Island was also a major marketplace for these types of wares, especially those manufactured in Bristol County. There was very little red earthenware production in Rhode Island, especially after the American Revolution. There were basically two documented red earthenware businesses operating in Rhode Island before 1790, one owned by Joseph Wilson (b. ca. 1735) in Providence and another operated by the Upton brothers in East Greenwich.

Joseph Wilson was an Essex County, Massachusetts trained potter, related to the eighteenth and nineteenth century Wilson family of potters in South Danvers (today known as Peabody), who traveled to Dedham, Massachusetts, and later Providence. He advertised on June 22, 1767 in the *Newport (Rhode Island) Mercury, "Joseph Wilson – potter at the North End of Providence Informs the Public that he can Supply them with Earthen Ware at a Cheap Rate, made in the best Manner and Glazed in the Same Way as Practised in Philadelphia – All Persons in this Town may be regularly supplied by Means of the Boats which constantly pass between this place and Providence."*

The wares made in Philadelphia during this period were viewed in many parts of America as the best and most fashionable in the country. It should not be a surprise to learn that potters used this demand to try and sell their products. To my knowledge, there is only one piece of surviving pottery known that is thought to have been manufactured by Wilson in Dedham, a slip decorated red earthenware pan now in the collection of the National Museum of American History in Washington, D.C. It was published in 1950 in Figure 26 in Massachusetts author Lura Woodside Watkins' (1897-1982) book, *Early New England Potters and Their Wares,* and dated in the center "*1764.*"

Interestingly, archaeologists from the University of Massachusetts at Boston excavated the remains of a slip decorated red earthenware pan a few summers ago, about forty miles west of Dedham in Grafton, Massachusetts. The pan was recovered from a mid-eighteenth century site, although, objects certainly could date from the 1760s. There are similarities in this

A Celebrated Industry

pan when compared to Wilson's known production, as well as wares made in Philadelphia, along with other areas.

Above) My nephew Jason holding a surviving late eighteenth or early nineteenth century slip decorated red earthenware dish a short distance from where it was made in Philadelphia.

Bottom) The dish compared to some locally made eighteenth century slip decorated red earthenware recovered by archaeologists in Philadelphia. (courtesy Archaeology at Independence)

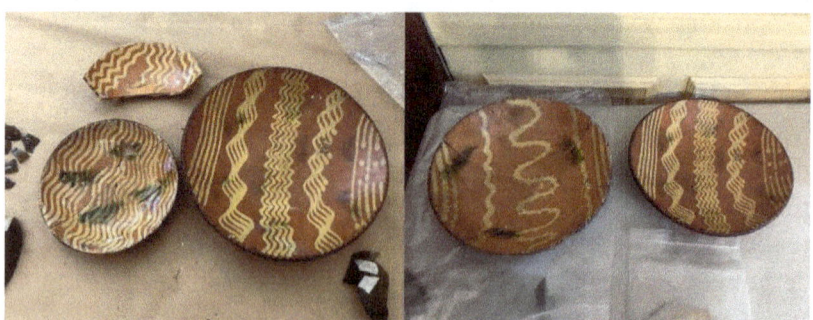

A Celebrated Industry

Eighteenth century slip decorated red earthenware pan attributed to Joseph Wilson in Dedham, Mass., dated in the center "1764." (courtesy National Museum of American History at the Smithsonian Institute)

A Celebrated Industry

Remains of a slip decorated red earthenware pan recovered from a mid-eighteenth century archaeological context in Grafton, Mass. (courtesy UMass Boston, Fiske Center for Archaeological Research)

The story of the Upton brothers is legendary today, seeing that they are thought to have also produced some prolific green glazed wares. But in most cases, archaeological evidence is lacking to prove what they may have produced versus the green glazed wares from Bristol County and elsewhere in southeastern Massachusetts.

When Dr. Daniel Howland Greene (1807-1886) published *History of the Town of East Greenwich and Adjacent Territory From 1677-1877* in the nineteenth century, he wrote, "*At the commencement of the Revolutionary War, a man by the name of Upton came from Nantucket to East Greenwich, and manufactured earthenware for a number of years. The pottery where the articles were made, and the kiln where they were baked, stood on the lot now occupied by the dwelling house of John Weeden, on the corner of King and Marlboro Street. The articles made there consisted of pans, bowls, plates, cups, and saucers.*

The clay for making those articles was brought by Quidnessett at a place called Gould's Mount, on the farm now belonging to Henry Waterman, and where great quantities of the same kind of clay remain. Shortly after the termination of the Revolutionary War, Mr. Upton returned to Nantucket, and no earthenware has been made here since."

However, current research has found that this pottery was operated by two brothers, Isaac (1736-1824) and Samuel Upton (1748-1819), who likely learned the potters craft while they were employed in Berkley, Massachusetts in the 1760s, a town that largely contributed to the well-known industry in Bristol County. They also had family ties to the industry in Essex County.

It is important to note that Isaac Upton's name is found in a circa 1757-1766 account book owned by Winterthur in Wilmington, Delaware, which was kept by Preserved Peirce (1736-1798), a merchant from Swansea, Massachusetts, who traded along the coast of Rhode Island and Connecticut. He sold wooden and pewter goods, pottery, and tools for craftsman and potters. Isaac's name is among the potters who Peirce purchased earthenware from in Berkley.

In spite of the Uptons remarkable history as Colonial New England potters, there is not a lot of information known about their East Greenwich business. Over the last century, there has been some pottery attributed to the Uptons, but some of these attributions are questioned today, seeing there is a lack of physical evidence to prove this information. The forms include skillfully thrown pitchers and refined teacups and saucers.

Based on archaeological evidence, a great deal of wares from Bristol County were shipped to Rhode Island in the eighteenth and nineteenth centuries, and some of the forms were probably like what the Uptons made, in such a way that it has created a great deal of confusion. But even so, it is believed (or known) that the Uptons did manufacture a vibrant green glaze, which is considered to be very similar to some of the prized green glazes produced in Bristol County, as well as elsewhere in southeastern Massachusetts and possibly Cape Cod.

The archaeology of the East Greenwich pottery also seems to be lacking, although, the remains of a large green glazed

A Celebrated Industry

jar was uncovered in the 1990s beneath an old barn in East Greenwich. The whereabouts of this jar is currently unknown, but it is thought to have been made at the Upton Pottery.

The sources used for attribution for the Upton wares is largely two articles written by Charles D. Cook; the first was published in the July 1925 quarterly issue of *Rhode Island Historical Society Collections* and the second was written for the January 1931 issue of *The Magazine Antiques*, titled "Early Rhode Island Pottery." Some of green pieces illustrated may have been made by the Uptons, while others are undoubtedly from elsewhere in New England.

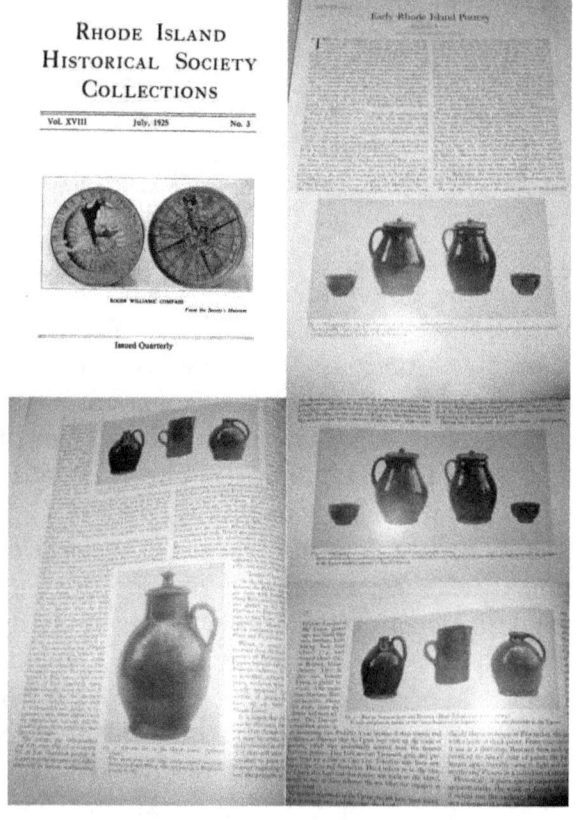

Articles were written by Charles D. Cook about Rhode Island pottery for the July 1925 quarterly issue of *Rhode Island Historical Society Collections* **and the January 1931 issue of The Magazine Antiques, titled, Early Rhode Island Pottery.**

A Celebrated Industry

Green glazed red earthenware teacup thought to have been made at the Upton Pottery in East Greenwich, R.I. It was published with this attribution in an article written by Charles D. Cook for the January 1931 issue of The Magazine Antiques, titled, Early Rhode Island Pottery, although the glaze also closely resembles a style recovered by Lura Woodside Watkins in Berkley, Bristol County, Mass. now at the Smithsonian Institute in Washington, D.C.; see Chapter 5, Figure 5.21. (courtesy Jeff & Holly Noordsy) Also see picture 307 for additional image.

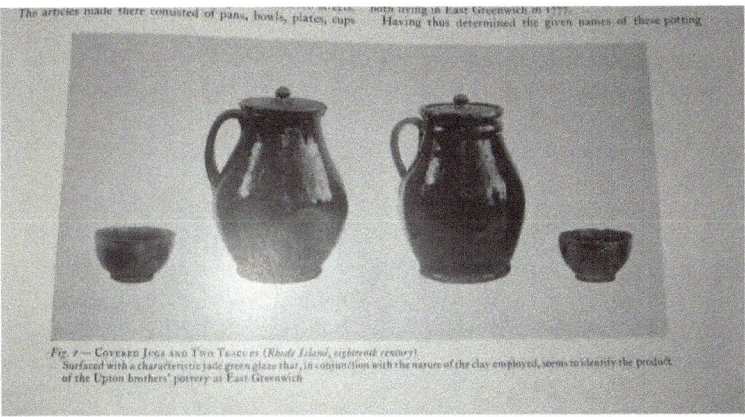

The teacup shown above as illustrated (far right) in Charles D. Cook's article in The Magazine Antiques. It was also published in Brian Cullity's exhibit catalog Slipped and Glazed: Regional American Redware.

A Celebrated Industry

Historically though, Rhode Island was a state dominated by domestic red earthenware exported from Bristol County and possibly parts of Connecticut in the late eighteenth and nineteenth century. It has been reported that the clay beds were not the same quality for red earthenware production when compared to other parts of New England.

Comparatively the wares manufactured in southeastern Massachusetts, Bristol County and Cape Cod were at the forefront of New England 's red earthenware industry. This was also an industry that was largely dominated by potters of English descent celebrating their Quaker faith. And because of the Quakerism in this region, it was often a job that was passed on through generation of family ownership and multiple family-run businesses. This may also account for why the forms and glazes were so masterfully produced since it was a skill that could be refined as it passed from one potter to the next.

However, production from this region was not exclusively based on English potters from the Quaker religion. There was also at least one prominent potter from Germany, and likely other potters who are not accounted for today, and perhaps even businesses that have been lost to history. As a result, there are some objects that survive today, but the location, potter, or business that they originated at is debatable. This book covers the better-known business, but it does not account for every business and every potter from southeastern Massachusetts, Bristol County and Cape Cod.

Probably an eighteenth century red earthenware handled pot possibly used for honey found in the Hingham, Mass. area. (courtesy Bill Taylor)

A Celebrated Industry

Eighteenth or early nineteenth century red earthenware jug possibly from southeastern Massachusetts.

Eighteenth or early nineteenth century slip decorated red earthenware jug possibly from southeastern Massachusetts. (courtesy Sam Herrup)

Late eighteenth or early nineteenth century red earthenware jar retaining a history of ownership in southeastern Mass., although the maker is not identified.

A Celebrated Industry

Late eighteenth or early nineteenth century red earthenware jar that is similar in manufacture to some objects produced in southeastern Massachusetts and Bristol County.

Late eighteenth or early nineteenth century red earthenware jar that is similar in manufacture to some objects produced in southeastern Massachusetts and Bristol County, as well as Essex County and by Peter Clark in Mass. and New Hampshire.

Late eighteenth or early nineteenth century red earthenware handled pot that is similar in manufacture to some objects produced in southeastern Massachusetts and Bristol County.

A Celebrated Industry

Late eighteenth or early nineteenth century red earthenware sander manufactured in New England and possibly related to the wares illustrated throughout this book. (courtesy Sam Herrup)

Late eighteenth or early nineteenth century small red earthenware jar that is similar in manufacture to some objects produced in southeastern Massachusetts and Bristol County, as well as locations elsewhere in New Engnland.

Late eighteenth or early nineteenth century red earthenware pitcher that is similar in manufacture to some objects produced in southeastern Massachusetts and Bristol County. The pitcher retains a history of ownership in South Natick, Mass. (courtesy Metropolitan Museum of Art)

A Celebrated Industry

(Top and Bottom Left) The origin of these jars (pictures above are from the same jar) is currently unknown, but certainly noteworthy when discussing the aesthetic appeal of coastal Massachusetts and New England red earthenware production. (courtesy Sam Herrup and Steve Corrigan)

A Celebrated Industry

Late eighteenth or early nineteenth century black glazed red earthenware jar. Manufacturer unknown, but it does share some similarities with wares made in southeastern Massachusetts and Bristol County. (courtesy Skinner)

Two separate views of a nineteenth century green glazed red earthenware vase typically associated with production in New England. There are a few of these known to exist today. (courtesy Lew Scranton and Skinner)

> Chapter 1

Eighteenth Century Red Earthenware Production in Abington and Quincy, Mass.

John Henry Benner (ca. 1727-1796), a potter born in Nidda, Hesse, Germany, immigrated to the American colonies as part of a wave of German craftsman, who joined settlements in Maine, Massachusetts, Pennsylvania, and North Carolina. He first settled in Phillips Head, Old Braintree (now Quincy), also known as Germantown and helped establish a business known as the Glassworks. A potter was needed to make the crucible to hold the molten glass.

As part of Lura Woodside Watkins' investigation of the Germantown settlement in Quincy for *Early New England Potters and Their Wares*, she discovered a red earthenware sherd adorned with a slip decorated tulip, presumed to be American made, and similar to wares made by German immigrant potters in places like Pennsylvania, Maryland, and North Carolina. This sherd is kept today at the National Museum of American History at the Smithsonian Institute in Washington, D.C.

In 1752, General Joseph Palmer (1716-1788) and Richard Cranch (1726-1811), brother-in-law of John Adams (1735-1826) and father of American jurist, William Cranch (1769-1855), were held by tenure of lease by a company interested in German immigration to create a planned manufacturing community in a section of Quincy known as Germantown. The land was to be settled in the 1750s by a group of glassmakers and weavers from

A Celebrated Industry

Germany. The planned community had failed by 1760, but the name has remained.

According to Watkins, *"Almost every authority of American ceramics has stated as a fact that pottery was made in the German colony in Quincy known as Germantown. Their reason for believing this to be so was that Judge William Cranch, a descendent of Richard Cranch, one of the proprietors of the eighteenth-century German glassworks and other manufacturers there, had picked up fragments of stoneware near the site of the enterprise. This I have done, also, and I have found sherds of slip decorated red earthenware near the shore. I cannot, however, obtain any real proof that pottery making was one of the Germantown industries."*

It also must be taken into consideration that the Colonial red earthenware industry in Charlestown, Massachusetts was New England's centralized pottery production center during this period, shipping red earthenware all over coastal New England, as far north as Canada and as far south as the Carolinas. The slip decorated red earthenware that Watkins recovered may have been produced in nearby Charlestown. Although, the sherd she recovered at the Smithsonian is unlike anything else known to have been produced in New England in the 1700s.

Figure 1.1 Red earthenware sherd adorned with a multicolor slip decorated tulip recovered by Lura Woodside Watkins in Germantown in Quincy, Mass. This may have been produced locally in the 1750s, and it is similar to slipware manufactured by other immigrant German potters working in places like Pennsylvania, Maryland and North Carolina. (courtesy National Museum of American History at the Smithsonian Institute)

A Celebrated Industry

Figure 1.2-1.4 Top) Surviving circa 1750 slip decorated handled bowl made in Charlestown, Mass. (Below) The pot shown with a Charlestown chamber pot and porringer recovered from a privy at the site of the Three Cranes Tavern in Charlestown. (courtesy Sam Herrup and City of Boston Archaeology Program)

"There is a list of male members of the community in 1757, which I (Watkins) have used in an attempt to discover in their land records whether any of them were potters, but the search

was fruitless, as an examination of documents in state archives. It seems likely that Judge Cranch's finds were merely household breakage, particularly in view of the fact that stoneware could not be made of local clay."

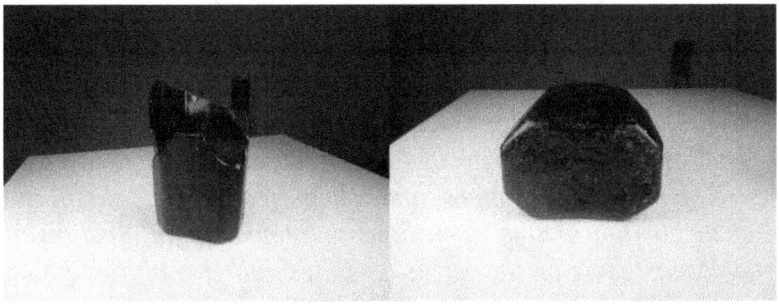

Figure 1.5-1.6 Eighteenth century glass recovered in Charlestown, Mass. probably made in Germantown in Quincy, Mass. (courtesy City of Boston Archaeology Department)

Around 1757-1758, Benner moved about ten miles south to Abington, Plymouth County, Massachusetts. He and his family lived in a cottage on the back part of the estate of Woodbridge Browne (1714-1783), son of Reverend Samuel Browne (1687-1749) and town clerk of Abington. That cottage may have stood between present day 325 Washington Street and 87 Nash Memorial Road. Records show that both John and his son served as Revolutionary War soldiers from Abington between 1776 and 1782.

Benner dug his clay on this land, which is now covered by the blacktop turnaround at the end of Nash Memorial Road. His kiln was behind what is now 112 Nash Memorial Road.

Benner threw his pottery on a foot-powered potter's wheel; he dug his own clay, ground it, cured it, and made it into a variety of utilitarian forms that were probably used by almost every family in town. Archaeological evidence kept at the Historical Society of Old Abington shows much of Benner's production was glazed only on the interior, sloshing the glaze rather than dipping it. The glaze colors include cream, mustard, a bright green, and various darker colors, like black and brown.

Watkins visited the site of this business in 1942, writing in *Early New England Potters and Their Wares*, "*Back of the ploughed portion of this open land, I found a small section of Benner's waste pile on the very edge of a small clay pit filled with water. The sherds recovered were for the most part similar to the work of our potters of English descent. The one notable exception was a fragment of a bowl or jar with slip stripings trailed horizontally on the outside. Much of the ware is of a brilliant red-orange color treated with splashings and dribblings of dark glaze.*"

Interestingly, a slip decorated bowl was recovered in Bourne on Cape Cod in Massachusetts thought to have possibly been manufactured in Charlestown (Figure 8.4), but Benner's slipware may have also been similar in technique. Fragments of similar bowls have also been recovered in Charlestown.

In the collection of the Dyer Memorial Library in Abington is a small teapot made by Benner that was obtained by the library from a descendent of Benner. The museum also owns a jug, a pan, a creamer, and a toy figure of a beaver, as well as a cat, also attributed to Benner. Interestingly, the jug is decorated in a vibrant multi-colored glaze – a similar glazed pot on the interior was recovered from a pre-1775 context in Charlestown. There is also a red earthenware porringer decorated with this type of glaze known, further embellished with some slip decoration.

The creamer is also of particular interest seeing the glaze is similar to glaze colors manufactured in Bristol County in the eighteenth and early nineteenth century so it must be taken into consideration that some wares thought to have been produced in Bristol County might have actually been made in Abington.

A Celebrated Industry

Benner died at the age of sixty-eight on January 16, 1796, leaving behind a legacy of eighteenth-century pottery production, where he is considered today as a master of his craft and a superior potter.

Figure 1.7 Eighteenth century red earthenware pitcher or creamer attributed to John Henry Benner in Abington, Mass. (courtesy The Dyer Memorial Library)

Figure 1.8 Likely an eighteenth century red earthenware pitcher or creamer possibly made by John Henry Benner in Abington, Mass. (courtesy Winterthur)

A Celebrated Industry

Figure 1.9-1.10 Small eighteenth century red earthenware teapot attributed to John Henry Benner in Abington, Mass. (courtesy The Dyer Memorial Library)

A Celebrated Industry

Figure 1.11 Red earthenware jug reportedly attributed to John Henry Benner in Abington, Mass. The manufacture of the handle is similar to the handle found on the teapot shown in Figures 1.9-1.10. (courtesy The Dyer Memorial Library)

Figure 1.12 (Right) Eighteenth century red earthenware pot recovered in Charlestown, Mass. decorated with a similar glaze on the interior as the jug. (courtesy The Dyer Memorial Library)

A Celebrated Industry

Figure 1.13 Eighteenth century slip decorated red earthenware porringer decorated with a very similar glaze as the jug reportedly made by John Henry Benner in Abington, Mass.; see Figures 1.11-1.12. (courtesy Tim Gould)

A Celebrated Industry

Figure 1.14 Eighteenth century red earthenware cat attributed to John Henry Benner in Abington, Mass. (courtesy The Dyer Memorial Library)

Figure 1.15 Eighteenth century red earthenware beaver attributed to John Henry Benner in Abington, Mass. (courtesy The Dyer Memorial Library)

A Celebrated Industry

Figure 1.16-1.17 Eighteenth century red earthenware pan attributed to John Henry Benner in Abington, Mass. (courtesy The Dyer Memorial Library)

A Celebrated Industry

Figure 1.18-1.19 Eighteenth century red earthenware kiln bricks and kiln furniture attributed to John Henry Benner in Abington, Mass. (courtesy The Dyer Memorial Library)

A Celebrated Industry

Figure 1.20-1.21 Red earthenware jug possibly manufactured by John Henry Benner in Abington, Mass. The images show the jug in two separate types of lighting. (courtesy Anthony Butera, Jr.)

A Celebrated Industry

Figure 1.22 Late eighteenth or early nineteenth century red earthenware jug found by Paul Decoste in Essex County, Mass. in the 1960s. Form is slightly similar to the jug pictured in Figures 1.20-1.21. (courtesy Paul DeCoste and Skinner)

A Celebrated Industry

Figure 1.23 Late eighteenth or early nineteenth century red earthenware jug most likely manufactured at the same business as the jug illustrated in Figures 1.20-1.21. (courtesy Jeffrey S. Evans & Associates)

Figure 1.24 Late eighteenth or early nineteenth century red earthenware jug similar in form to the jugs illustrated in Figures 1.20-1.21.

Figure 1.25 Small red earthenware creamer possibly related to John Henry Benner's production. (courtesy Sotheby's)

A Celebrated Industry

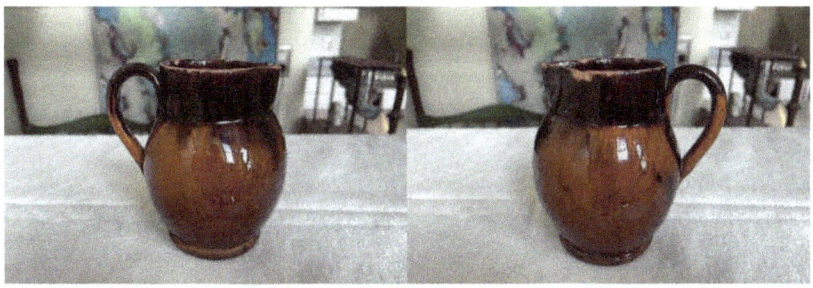

Figure 1.26-1.27 Eighteenth century red earthenware pitcher found in the Abington, Mass. area that matches the pitcher illustrated in Figure 1.7 that is attributed to John Henry Benner. (courtesy Bill Taylor)

Figure 1.28 Eighteenth or early nineteenth century red earthenware pitcher that shares some similarities to John Henry Benner's production, although it is unknown if this piece is related or from another manufacturer. (courtesy Historic Deerfield)

A Celebrated Industry

Figure 1.29 Red earthenware creamer and porringer possibly related to John Henry Benner's production. (courtesy John McInnis and a private collector) Note: A similar small pitcher or creamer also sold in Crocker Farm's March 25, 2017 sale lot number 252.

A Celebrated Industry

Benner Archaeology at the Smithsonian Institute

Figure 1.30 Various red earthenware artifacts collected by Lura Woodside Watkins at the site of the John Henry Benner Pottery in Abington, Mass. in 1942. (courtesy National Museum of American History at the Smithsonian Institute in Washington, D.C.)

A Celebrated Industry

Figure 1.31 Various red earthenware artifacts collected by Lura Woodside Watkins at the site of the John Henry Benner Pottery in Abington, Mass. in 1942. (courtesy National Museum of American History at the Smithsonian Institute in Washington, D.C.)

A Celebrated Industry

Figure 1.32 Various slip-decorated red earthenware artifacts collected by Lura Woodside Watkins at the site of the John Henry Benner Pottery in Abington, Mass. in 1942. (courtesy National Museum of American History at the Smithsonian Institute in Washington, D.C.)

Figure 1.33 Various red earthenware artifacts collected by Lura Woodside Watkins at the site of the John Henry Benner Pottery in Abington, Mass. in 1942. (courtesy National Museum of American History at the Smithsonian Institute in Washington, D.C.)

Figure 1.34 Kiln furniture collected by Lura Woodside Watkins at the site of the John Henry Benner Pottery in Abington, Mass. in 1942. (courtesy National Museum of American History at the Smithsonian Institute in Washington, D.C.)

> Chapter 2

The Wares Manufactured in Braintree, Mass. and Lyndeborough, New Hampshire

Traditionally, treasure maps consist of sketchy outlines with a large "X" that marks the burial spot of hidden treasure. Factual or fictional, treasure maps are not traditionally associated with eighteenth or nineteenth century American utilitarian potters. However, a recently discovered nineteenth century document has unintentionally revealed the location of one of an eighteenth or early nineteenth century New Hampshire pottery – that of Peter Clark (1743-1826) in Lyndeborough, New Hampshire.

Recently, a group of ephemera became available and some of those documents were associated with Peter Clark, who was a potter employed in Braintree, Massachusetts from circa 1763 to 1775.

In his diary, Clark records that he left for Lyndeborough on January 25, 1775, and taking with him an early coastal Massachusetts potter's style. That included technique, form, glaze, and incised decoration, which he probably learned in Essex County, Massachusetts. Clark's New Hampshire products can also be mistaken for objects made in southeastern Massachusetts today and Bristol County, which also partially possess an Essex County background. Among the techniques found in both coastal Massachusetts and with Clark's production is a large round foot at the base of objects, banded incised decoration and some glazes similar to those from Bristol County.

A Celebrated Industry

In her book, *Early New England Potters and Their Wares*, Massachusetts author Lura Woodside Watkins writes, *"Peter Clark was running a pottery in Braintree as early as 1763. He came from a Danvers, Massachusetts family that moved to Braintree before he was born. He kept up his Danvers associations and was probably trained there, too. Clark even went back to Danvers in 1772 for clay. This was doubtless white clay for slip decorating, as redware clay was abundant in Braintree. In 1768, he was selling his wares in Hingham, Massachusetts and elsewhere in that vicinity."*

Clark's use of slip is largely unknown today and his reasons for moving north are not well-documented. But I suspect that he moved to south central New Hampshire in search of opportunity. Coastal Massachusetts was overflowing with red earthenware potters – and he may have found that there was too much competition in southeastern Massachusetts. In fact, there were dozens of potter's businesses located to the north and south of Boston. An important potter's industry was also active in Charlestown, which employed a number of successful potters. This industry ended abruptly on June 17, 1775 at the Battle of Bunker Hill; however, that was after Clark had already moved to New Hampshire. Coastal New Hampshire was also well-supplied with utilitarian pottery from local potters and wares shipped from parts of coastal Massachusetts. But during the Revolutionary period, inland communities in places like central Massachusetts, central New Hampshire, Vermont, and Maine multiplied and grew in size.

It seems that Peter Clark, good businessman that he was, must have noticed the expanding population that had moved inland, away from New England's coast. He knew that, like all communities, they needed good supplies of utilitarian pottery. This may have well been the reason why he moved to New Hampshire where he could better support his family. He also may have feared for his family's safety with the growing turmoil in coastal Massachusetts just before the American Revolution.

Clark's diary is fascinating. Watkins cited it as being owned in 1950 by Mrs. Joseph N. Robinson of Malden, Massachusetts, but its whereabouts is unknown to me today. He did not confine it to keeping record of his red earthenware business, but he also recorded events for thirty years, such as the entry on April 19th, 1775, *"the fight began at Concord."* The diary also contains the records of Clark's service during the American Revolution, where he served as a captain and a major. Afterwards, Clark was actively involved with Lyndeborough's political system, which may have helped his pottery business prosper, as he owned his own store in Lyndeborough. He also served as a deacon to the local church.

There was a document in that group of ephemera that really helped define the location of Peter Clark's property in the nineteenth century. The document proclaimed that the property of the late-Sarah G. Goodridge in Francestown, New Hampshire would be divided at public auction in 1845 to pay off existing debts. The area's land was described, as, *"...then running easterly Daniel Proctor's land to the land of Nathan Brown then northerly by Mr. Brown's land until it comes to the road leading to the turnpike then running westerly by the road until it comes to Peter Clark's land."* This important document also came with a hand-drawn map that showed the location of Peter Clark's property. It is unclear if this map was drawn for the auction itself, but these documents have survived together for many years.

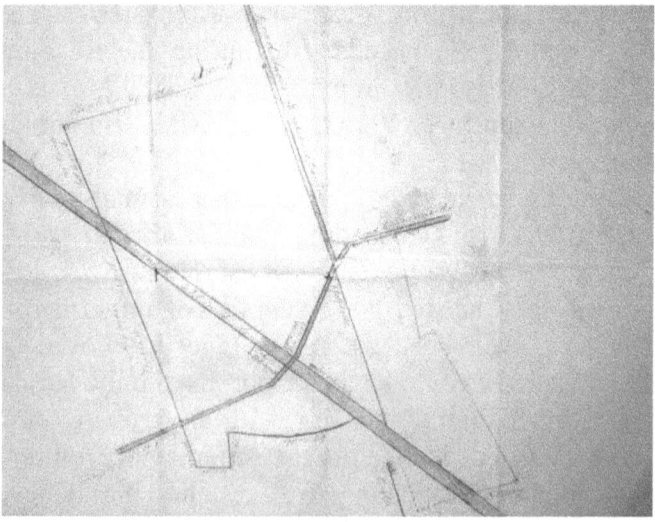

Figure 2.1 Map showing the location of Peter Clark's pottery in Lyndeborough, New Hampshire. (courtesy Mark Newton)

A Celebrated Industry

A recent investigation of the land shown on the map yielded a collection of sherds, kiln wasters, kiln bricks and kiln furniture. Whether this was actually the site of the kiln or an area where the Clarks disposed of kiln waste is yet to be determined, but the waste is almost certainly from the Clark pottery.

It does not tell us anything new or surprising but confirms that Peter Clark's family was similar to any other late eighteenth or early nineteenth century red earthenware potter's business in central or northern New England. The company produced all the traditional forms that were made by any other potter during the same period: Crocks, pots, pans, jugs, jars, pitchers, cups, and mugs – everything that the local community required for daily life.

A likely prominent example of Clark's eighteenth-century production is owned by Old Sturbridge Village in Sturbridge, Massachusetts. The form is a double-handled dark glazed jug with a client's inscription, *"Oliver Laurence / Lyndeborough, New Hampshire / October 18, 1786."* Without this inscription, the form of the jug could easily be interpreted as nineteenth century production.

Figure 2.2 Eighteenth century double handled red earthenware jug likely made by Peter Clark in Lyndeborough, N.H., inscribed, *Oliver Laurence / Lyndeborough, New Hampshire / October 18, 1786."* **(courtesy Old Stubridge Village)**

After Peter Clark's death in 1826, the family continued producing traditional styles of red earthenware. There is no specific evidence that proves exactly how long the Lyndeborough production continued, but it is believed to have operated well-into the 1850s or the 1860s.

Fortunately, the Clark family tradition did not end in Lyndenborough. The family had expanded about thirty-five miles northeast to the state capital in Concord, New Hampshire. Peter Clark's son, Daniel Clark (1768-1828), established the Concord business in the city's Millville neighborhood. Daniel's sons would eventually transform this company in the second half of the nineteenth century.

The Millville operation employed traveling potters and apprentices, so it was apparently larger than the pottery in Lyndeborough. It seems that the Concord business was also more innovative in its production: There were attempts to reproduce eighteenth century English products; they also manufactured pieces in support of both political parties during presidential campaigns, objects celebrating the centennial, as well as toy figures, spittoons and art vases often painted with decorative designs. Comparatively all of these objects are considered rare today.

In some ways though, the Clark family potteries in Lyndeborough and Concord are overshadowed today by the Osborn family in New Hampshire. The fact is that both families shared equal involvement in the New Hampshire pottery industry. The Osborns originated in South Danvers (today known as Peabody), Massachusetts in the 1730s, but family members eventually branched out into places like Gonic, Loudon, Boscowan and Dover, New Hampshire in the 1800s. They were seeking the same opportunity that Peter Clark sought in 1775. The Osborn family is generally viewed as possibly the most important family of potters in New Hampshire with the Clarks as an afterthought. However, this idea needs to change. The Clarks came before the Osborns and established a family legacy that lasted well into the 1880s. This was a milestone in itself since small potteries in New England had vanished by this time due to the industry's transformation that occurred with the Industrial Revolution, evolving technology, the Arts and Crafts Movement

A Celebrated Industry

and the demand for stoneware, which was eventually viewed as a superior product.

Figure 2.3 Nineteenth century red earthenware pitcher made by James L. Osborn (1833-1893) in Gonic, N.H. Inscribed on the base "J.L. Osborn / 1874."

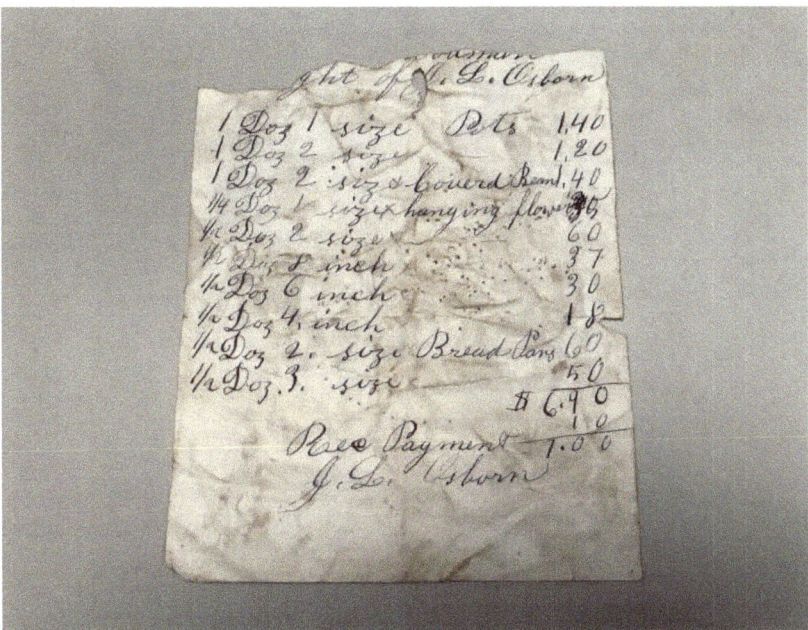

Figure 2.4a Receipt for an order of earthenware signed by James L. Osborn (1833-1893) from the Gonic, N.H. pottery, likely circa 1850-1885. (courtesy Private Collection). See Figures 2.4b and 2.4c for another signed piece of pottery made by James L. Osborn.

A Celebrated Industry

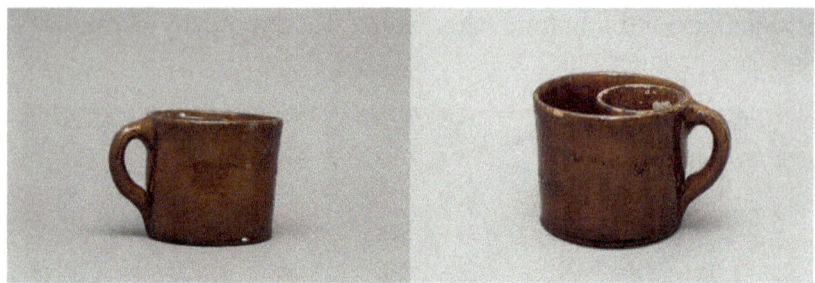

Figure 2.4b-2.4c Nineteenth century red earthenware mug inscribed "James L. Osborn 1877 / Gonic." (courtesy Historic Deerfield)

A Celebrated Industry

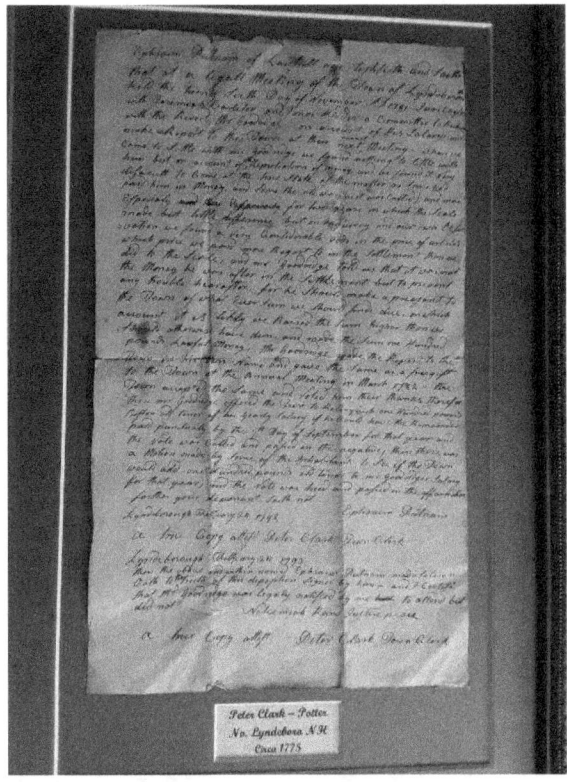

Figure 2.5 Legal document probably written and signed by Peter Clark, dated "1793." (courtesy Mark Newton)

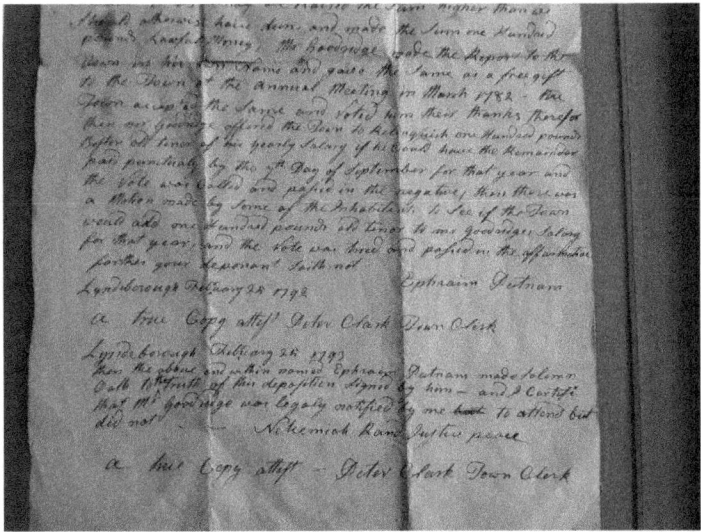

A Celebrated Industry

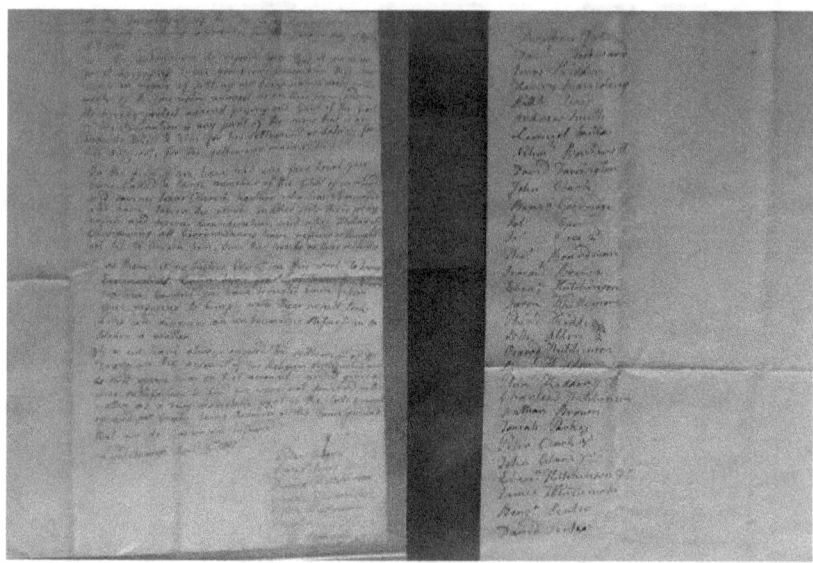

Figure 2.6 A document likely written by Peter Clark trying to convince the town of Lyndeborough, New Hampshire not to hire a preacher. Clark's name is first among the signatures so it is likely that he wrote it. The back (show to the right abovove) also includes a couple of signatures from Clark's sons. (courtesy Mark Newton)

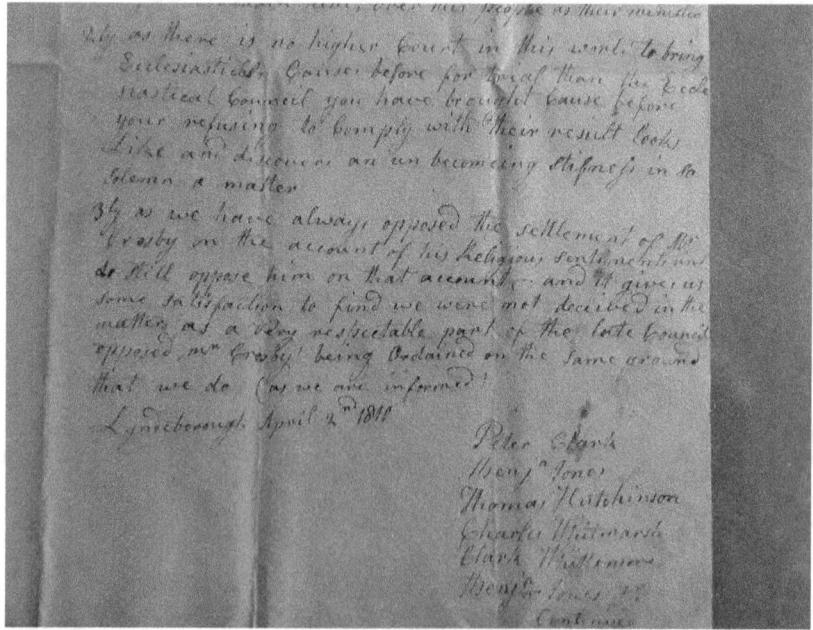

A Celebrated Industry

Peter Clark is a significant name in respect to the eighteenth-century New England potter's industry. He was a landmark potter, who began his career well before the Revolutionary War and who lived within fifteen miles of the events that led up to the American Revolution, such as the Boston Massacre, the Boston Tea Party, and the Intolerable Acts. Even though not a lot is known about his Braintree production today, this production must have been similar to what he manufactured in New Hampshire. He was also located a short distance from the Charlestown potter's industry, which he must have witnessed.

However, his role in New Hampshire is justly important since it was his family who helped lay the foundation for central New Hampshire's potter's industry, which ultimately prospered in the nineteenth century. The Clark pottery was eventually surrounded by a number of other small potteries throughout inland New Hampshire. Peter Clark was truly a groundbreaking potter who had the foresight to leave Massachusetts in the 1700s in search of opportunity. This was not a move that most other potters dared to make until the decades that followed the outcome of the American Revolution.

Figure 2.7 Some of the artifacts collected at the site of the Peter Clark Pottery in Lyndeborough, N.H. (courtesy Mark Newton)

A Celebrated Industry

Figure 2.8 Red earthenware jar thought to have been made by Peter Clark before 1775 in Braintree, Mass., but more likely from Lyndeborough, N.H.. (courtesy National Museum of American History at the Smithsonian Institute, Lura Woodside Watkins Collection)

Figure 2.9 Late eighteenth or early nineteenth century red earthenware jar attributed to Peter Clark in Lyndeborough, New Hampshire. (courtesy The Bennington Museum)

A Celebrated Industry

Figure 2.10 Late eighteenth or early nineteenth century red earthenware jar attributed to Peter Clark in Lyndeborough, New Hampshire. (courtesy New Hampshire Historical Society)

A Celebrated Industry

Figure 2.11a Late eighteenth or early nineteenth century red earthenware jar attributed to the Peter Clark Pottery. (courtesy Jim Mahoney)

Figure 2.11b Late eighteenth or early nineteenth century red earthenware jars attributed to the Peter Clark Pottery. (courtesy Historic Deerfield)

A Celebrated Industry

Figure 2.12 Late eighteenth or early nineteenth century red earthenware jar likely made at the Peter Clark Pottery in Lyndeborough, N.H. (courtesy Lyman Allyn Art Museum)

Figure 2.13 Late eighteenth or early nineteenth century red earthenware jar likely made at the Peter Clark Pottery in Lyndeborough, N.H,. although it was found in Rhode Island.

A Celebrated Industry

Figure 2.14 Red earthenware jars that exhibit characteristics of Peter Clark's production as well as potteries throughout coastal Massachusetts.

Figure 2.15 Red earthenware handled pot with its original lid that exhibits characteristics of Peter Clark's production as well as potteries throughout coastal Massachusetts. (courtesy Sam Herrup)

A Celebrated Industry

Figure 2.16-2.17 While there is no archaeological evidence, this style of jar has been previously attributed to southeastern Massachusetts, however, it also closely resembles production from the Clark family in Lyndeborough, New Hampshire, circa late eighteenth and early nineteenth century.

A Celebrated Industry

Figure 2.18 More examples of the type of jar shown in Figures 2.16-2.17. (courtesy Northeast Auctions)

Figure 2.19 Another example of the type of jar shown in Figures 2.16-2.17, but without handles. (courtesy Northeast Auctions)

A Celebrated Industry

Figure 2.20 Another example of the type of jar shown in Figure 2.16-2.17. (courtesy John Sideli)

Figure 2.21 Late eighteenth or early nineteenth century red earthenware jars likely made at the Peter Clark pottery in Lyndeborough, N.H., although the jar in the front does possibly have an eighteenth century look to it, based on known eighteenth century production from coastal Massachusetts. The jar shown to the far left was previously owned by Robesonia, Pennsylvania potter Lester Breininger (1935-2011).

Figure 2.22 Late eighteenth or early nineteenth century red earthenware jar attributed to Peter Clark and previously owned by Charles D. Cook. (courtesy Skinner)

Figure 2.23 Late eighteenth or early nineteenth century red earthenware jar probably made in Lyndeborough, N.H., and likely related to those illustrated in Figure 2.21. (courtesy Skinner)

A Celebrated Industry

Figure 2.24-2.29 All objects that exhibit incising similar to that used by Peter Clark, although, most of these pieces are unrelated. The flowerpot was recovered from an eighteenth century context at the Narbonnne House in Salem, Mass. The jar below that is inscribed "John Dunes / keep it fore you sake / September first 1835." (photos courtesy Peabody Essex Museum, National Park Service Narbonne House, John McInnis, Old Sturbridge Village and the National Museum of American History at the Smithsonian Institute)

A Celebrated Industry

Figure 2.30 Possibly an eighteenth century red earthenware handled pot attributed to Essex County, Mass., later used as a butter churn and decorated with similar incising like Clark used. Illustrated in picture 14 in Early New England Potters and Their Wares. (courtesy Peabody Historical Society)

Figure 2.31 Eighteenth century incised red earthenware sherd recovered from Harvard Yard at Harvard University. (courtesy Peabody Museum of Archaeology and Ethnology)

A Celebrated Industry

Peter Clark Archaeology at the Smithsonian Institute

Figure 2.32-2.34 Red earthenware sherds and kiln furniture collected by Lura Woodside Watkins in 1940 related to Peter Clark's production in New Hampshire. (courtesy National Museum of American History at the Smithsonian Institute)

A Celebrated Industry

> Chapter 3

The Bradford Family Pottery in Kingston, Mass.

The Bradford family's contribution to the southeastern Massachusetts red earthenware industry is a lesser-known story today, but certainly just as prominent as any other business operating in this region, especially after the American Revolution.

The origin of the Bradford family pottery can be traced back to John Bradford (1732-1818), who reportedly began producing bricks and likely red earthenware sometime around 1750 on his property in Kingston, Massachusetts, a small coastal community in Plymouth County, neighboring Plymouth, Massachusetts to the north. Furthermore, this family's fame actually emerged in the seventeenth century, seeing that they are direct descendants of William Bradford (1590-1657), a founder and longtime Governor of the Plymouth Colony settlement. Kingston is also strategically located for this type of business, since the land route from Plymouth to Boston traveled directly through Kingston, conveying a pottery business an easy shipping route for communities along that road.

Figure 3.1 William Bradford (1590-1657)

While not a lot of information is known about this early production, it is likely that John Bradford's son Stephen (1771-1837) and nephew Noah (1761-1832) learned the potter's trade from him. They both went on to have illustrious careers in the

Massachusetts pottery industry, but some of this history seems to have been forgotten through time.

As it may be, Lura Woodside Watkins appears to have been the first scholar to have published academically about the Bradfords in Kingston. But more recently, Martha L. Sulya wrote a 131-page report in 2015 about pottery production in Kingston, as part of her master's Theses for the University of Massachusetts at Boston, titled, *Ubiquitous and Unfamiliar: Earthenware Pottery Production Techniques and the Bradford Family Pottery of Kingston, MA.*

According to Sulya, *"It was Stephen Bradford, his son Stephen Bradford Junior (1807-1866), and grandson Orrin Bradford (1839-1890) who made earthenware pottery along Bridgewater Road in Kingston. Stephen Senior is identified as a potter when he purchased land in 1798 from his father, and by the time John sold Stephen Senior the rights to dig and transport clay from the family property in 1803, Stephen had also purchased adjoining lots from various relatives.*

Stephen Senior was well-established as a potter by the time his father sold him the family homestead in 1810. Stephen Junior worked with his father until his death in 1837 and thereafter continued to produce pottery. Most historians have then surmised that the pottery closed during Stephen Junior's life; however, documentary evidence identifies Orrin as a potter before and after his father's death in 1867. Rather than being completely abandoned, the pottery may have been just one source of family income along with a sawmill, a grist mill and agriculture."

A notable characteristic found with wares manufactured at the Bradford Pottery in Kingston is the use of various coggle decorations, some of which may very well have been unique designs for red earthenware production in New England. A great deal of this production, along with wasters, sherds, kiln bricks, kiln furniture, raw clay and raw glaze were discovered in 1996, when archaeologists Connie Crosby, Steven Pendery and a team of volunteers were involved with an eight-day archaeology dig at the site of Stephen Bradford's house in Kingston. These artifacts are kept today at Plimoth Plantation in Plymouth.

A Celebrated Industry

Much of the recovered artifacts also support the evidence found in sherds that I have studied at the National Museum of American History at the Smithsonian Institute in Washington, D.C. These sherds were discovered by Watkins in 1945 at the Bradford house; to my knowledge, she was the first scholar to visit this property in search of information about the company.

But my excitement certainly grew, when I visited the Smithsonian in June of 2018 to compare some of the sherds adorned with a specific type of coggle decoration to the decoration found on a colorfully glazed pitcher, which I had obtained a few summers before. The pitcher had resided in a longtime pottery collection assembled by the late Massachusetts collector Earl Curry.

As my nephew Jason held up sherd after sherd inside the storage room at the Smithsonian, that housed all the archaeology from domestic potters, and placed the coggle found on those sherds directly next to the coggle decoration on the pitcher - I realized that I was holding an example of red earthenware made at the Bradford Pottery in Kingston, circa 1800-1840. However, this was just the start of it because I also realized that this pitcher very likely served as proof in identifying the origin of the pitchers that sold in the Huntington Collection in Maine nearly forty-five years earlier. When placed in a lineup, the forms of these pitchers are all very similar, as are the glazes. These unusual glazes may also serve as proof in identifying the origin of a privately owned large ovoid red earthenware lidded jar (Figures 3.10-3.13), which demonstrates characteristics in its form, also found with pottery produced in this section of Massachusetts.

Based on this evidence, it would seem that some of the wares made in Kingston are similar to some of the objects manufactured about thirty-five miles southwest at the well-known industry along the Taunton River in Bristol County, Massachusetts. Consequently, the Bradfords in Kingston must have produced all the typical utilitarian forms, common to red earthenware production in coastal Massachusetts in the eighteenth and nineteenth centuries.

Another aspect of production I noticed when reviewing the sherds at the National Museum of American History was the use of three colored glazes. The typical colors used in this pattern were black and cream on top of a dark raspberry colored body. At the time of seeing this evidence, I quickly realized that some of these sherds had come from an ovoid jar, and that they truly resembled a type of jar generally attributed to Maine today (Figures 4.29-4.31), even though the exact pottery in Maine has never been explained with archaeological evidence. I now firmly believe that these type of jars and related pieces were also made by the Bradfords.

A sherd that could also very well be related to these jars that matches the glaze style was also recovered within a late eighteenth and early nineteenth century archaeological context in the backyard of the circa 1721 Samuel Bell (b. 1695) House in Salem, Massachusetts (Figures 4.31-4.33). It was recovered alongside various imported European ceramics, most of which were from an English origin, locally produced red earthenware from the Peabody area and what could be the remains of a black glazed teapot from Philadelphia. Salem was a major port during this period so some of these objects may have arrived in the city through Salem's maritime trade. It is difficult to say who may have occupied the house when this object was discovered, seeing that the property went through a number of ownership changes in the early 1800s.

It should also be taken into account that the Bradford Pottery in Kingston was a multigenerational business, and there may have been apprentices and other potters employed over the years, resulting in some differences found in the various forms, handles, etc. But the similarities do not stop here. In fact, Noah Bradford had learned the potter's craft in Kingston, and he may have worked with his cousin Stephen Senior in the early nineteenth century, but he eventually relocated elsewhere in Massachusetts. He established his own business in West Barnstable on Cape Cod, possibly based on an opportunity he had noticed from wares reportedly shipped from Kingston to that part of the state (Chapter 7).

Interestingly, it should also be noted that some of the known production in Kingston is comparable to wares manufactured by Peter Clark in Braintree and Lyndeborough, New Hampshire.

A Celebrated Industry

Watkins described some of the archaeology as, *"The few fragments recovered on the site show a style slightly different from that of Danvers pottery. Pots glazed on the inside only were a common item, as elsewhere, but were peculiar in having an impressed decoration effected by a cogglewheel a little distance below the rim. The Bradfords made a great variety of flowerpots, plain and fancy, some with a green glaze."*

Some of these types of flowerpots made by the Bradfords are owned by the Jones River Village Historical Society and displayed in the Major John Bradford (1653-1736) House Museum in Kingston (Figure 3.3-3.4). Related archaeological evidence has also been recovered at the site of another Bradford family pottery in West Barnstable in Cape Cod, probably within a circa 1820s context (Chapter 8). Archaeology has also revealed that this green glaze was similar to some of the green glazed wares manufactured in Bristol County.

In fact, among the nineteenth century archaeological evidence recovered in Charlestown, Massachusetts is a green glazed flowerpot rim sherd (Figure 3.5a-3.5b) that closely resembles archaeology found at the site of the Bradford Pottery on Cape Cod (Chapter 8), although, this certainly may also represent the green glazed wares produced in Kingston or even Bristol County.

Figure 3.2 Major John Bradford (1653-1736) House in Kingston, Mass. This house was a popular subject illustrated on various postcards in the 1900s, and it also displays a selection of flowerpots attributed to the Bradford Pottery in Kingston (see Figure 3.3-3.4)

A Celebrated Industry

Figure 3.3 Collection of wares manufactured by the Bradfords in Kingston, Mass., including a selection of green glazed flowerpots and saucers very similar to those discussed in Chapter 8. (courtesy Jones River Village Historical Society)

Figure 3.4 Some of the green glazed flowerpots and saucers manufactured by the Bradfords in Kingston, Mass. displayed at the Major John Bradford House. (courtesy Jones River Village Historical Society)

A Celebrated Industry

Figure 3.5a and 3.5b Remains of a green glazed red earthenware crimped rim, most likely from a flowerpot or saucer recovered in Charlstown, Mass. (courtesy City of Boston Archaeology Department)

A Celebrated Industry

Figure 3.6 Late eighteenth or early nineteenth century red earthenware pitcher attributed to the Bradford Pottery in Kingston, Mass. The attribution is based on archaeological evidence collected by Lura Woodside Watkins at the site of the pottery kept at the National Museum of American History at the Smithsonian Institute in Washington, D.C. (courtesy Private Collection)

Figure 3.7 Another view of the pitcher. (courtesy Sam Herrup)

A Celebrated Industry

Figure 3.8 Late eighteenth or early nineteenth century red earthenware jug very possibly made at the Bradford Pottery in Kingston, Mass. See Figure 3.9 for more information.

Figure 3.9 The handle found on the jug (Right) is nearly identical to the handle on the pitcher (Left) also shown in Figures 3.6 and 3.7.

A Celebrated Industry

Figure 3.10 Late eighteenth or early nineteenth century red earthenware jar believed to have been produced at the Bradford Pottery in Kingston, Mass. The jar's original lid is seen in the background. (courtesy Private Collection)

Figure 3.11 Another view of the jar and lid. (courtesy Sam Herrup)

A Celebrated Industry

Figure 3.12-3.13 Two pitchers and a jar all thought to be have been manufactured at the Bradford Pottery in Kingston, Mass. The attribution for the pitchers is based on archaeological evidence. See Chapter 4 for more information.

Archaeology of the Joseph Howland (ca. 1640-1704) Homesite on Howland Lane on Rocky Nook peninsula in Kingston, Mass.

A notable Colonial archaeological site in southeastern Massachusetts is Rocky Nook, a neighborhood in Kingston, Massachusetts. The neighborhood sits on a small peninsula of land on Kingston Bay, where the Jones River meets the Atlantic Ocean. This is also where John Howland (1592-1672/73) and his wife Elizabeth Tilley (1607-1687) lived from 1639 until his death in 1673. Four of their youngest children – Ruth, Jabez, Joseph and Isaac, were born in this home. Although Joseph Howland (ca. 1640-1704) eventually built a house across the street probably in the 1660s or 1670s soon after he and Elizabeth Southworth (b. 1647) married.

However, after Joseph's death in 1704, the house was passed onto his son James (1669-1738), who perhaps continued to live in the house with his family until it sold to Captain Benjamin Lothrop (1704-1787) in 1735.

Recent archaeology of the homesite conducted by the University of Virginia and the Plymouth Archaeological Rediscovery Project has uncovered some domestic slip decorated red earthenware. It is certainly possible that these artifacts may represent pottery manufactured at the industry in Charlestown, Massachusetts or even another manufacturer, but they also may represent John Bradford's earliest production in Kingston.

Figure 3.14 Sketch of the John Howland homesite on Rocky Nook peninsula in Kingston, Mass. (courtesy The Pilgrim John Howland Society)

A Celebrated Industry

Figure 3.15 The Joseph Howland homesite on Rocky Nook peninsula in Kingston, Mass. A memorial rock reads "Historic site of the 1676 home of Joseph Howland who lived here until his death in 1703/04. He was the son of John Howland a passenger on the Mayflower who purchased this property in 1638. Erected in 1963 by the Pilgrim John Howland Society."

Figure 3.16 Various types of red earthenware recovered from the Joseph Howland homesite on Rocky Nook peninsula in Kingston, Mass., although this may represent Benjamin Lothrop's occupancy of the property. John Bradford was also thought to be producing red earthenware near this site in Kingston around this period as well. Among the forms is a milk pan illustrated bottom right. (courtesy Plymouth Archaeological Rediscovery Project)

> Chapter 4

The Archaeology of the Kingston Pottery

A lot of archaeology survives today from the Bradford family pottery in Kingston, Massachusetts, where the site of the pottery was first visited in 1945 by Massachusetts author Lura Woodside Watkins (1897-1982). Archaeologists also excavated the site in 1996, where this archaeology is now kept at Plimouth Plantation in Plymouth, Massachusetts.

A few years ago, I studied the archaeology collected by Watkins at the National Museum of American History at the Smithsonian Institute in Washington, D.C., and it was revealing to see a wide variety of cogglewheel decorations applied just below the rim on a number of sherds. These decorations matched those found on a variety of surviving colorfully glazed pitchers that are known today, although, the business that these pieces originated has never been identified. There are other forms known that are decorated with other types of cogglewheel impressions that are also represented in the archaeology, and these pieces may represent production from the Bradfords as well.

It was certainly amazing to study this archaeology, seeing that the Bradfords were a prominent family business that has been somewhat overlooked through time. The red earthenware they produced was incredibly skilled, while they also decorated their wares in a wide variety of glazes.

Among those glazes was a group of three-color glazed sherds from jars that I describe as being decorated with raspberry, cream, and black colors. These sherds closely resemble two known jars and a pitcher (Figures 4.29-4.31 and 4.34), also of an origin where the business has never been identified. I suspect that even more information about this business will come to light as more pieces become known and more information becomes available about this very important company.

Nonetheless, the identified recovered forms include chamber pots, cups, flowerpots, milk pans, mugs, pitchers, plates, various pots and even some slipware.

I will note though, that the use of glaze colors by the Bradfords in Kingston seems to be comparable to wares manufactured by some of the country potters in Maine, who often decorated their wares in very colorful glazes. But the Bradfords production in Kingston also seems to be indicative of the industry in southeastern Massachusetts, Bristol County and Cape Cod.

Figure 4.1 Photograph from 1896 showing Stephen Bradford Senior's (1771-1837) house in Kingston, Mass. that he built in 1804. The archaeology of this site in 1996 was a result of a brick house that had been demolished in order to create a cranberry bog. The demolition and removal of topsoil revealed an abundance of kiln waste and ceramic artifacts. (courtesy Kingston Public Library)

Figure 4.2 1857 map showing the Bradford neighborhood on Bridgewater Road in Kingston, Mass. (courtesy Beverly Booth, Kingston Public Library)

A Celebrated Industry

Figure 4.3 Bradford house lot, September 1996. (courtesy Plimouth Plantation)

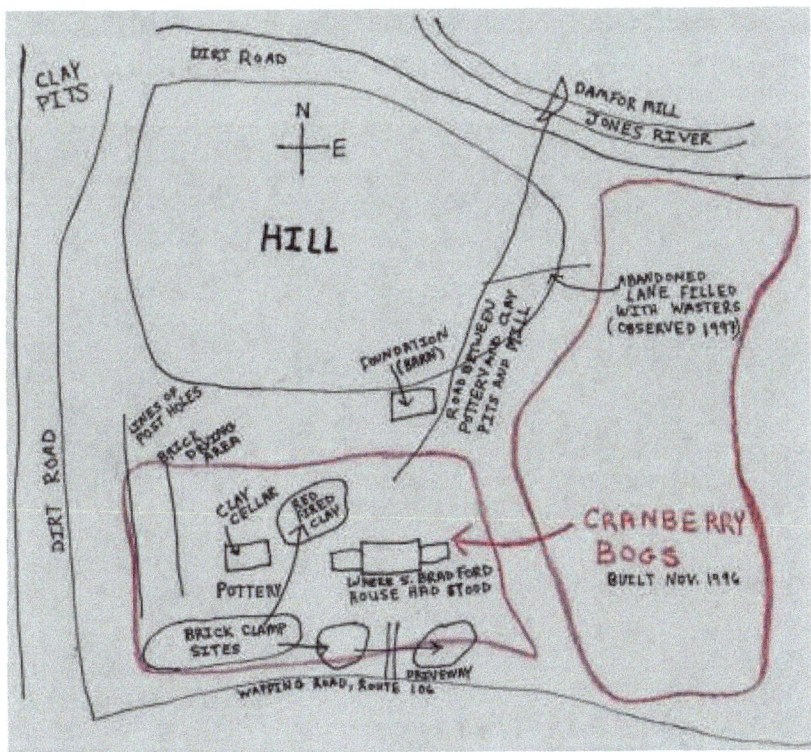

Figure 4.4 Hand-drawn map of Bradford Pottery site, 1996. (courtesy Michael Burrey)

A Celebrated Industry

Figure 4.5 My nephew Jason at the National Museum of American History at the Smithsonian Institute in Washington, D.C.

Figure 4.6 Various red earthenware sherds collected at the site of the Bradford Pottery in Kingston, Mass. (courtesy National Museum of American History at the Smithsonian Institute)

A Celebrated Industry

Figure 4.7 Various cogglewheel decorated red earthenware sherds collected at the site of the Bradford Pottery in Kingston, Mass. (courtesy National Museum of American History at the Smithsonian Institute)

Figure 4.8 Various cogglewheel decorated red earthenware sherds collected at the site of the Bradford Pottery in Kingston, Mass. (courtesy National Museum of American History at the Smithsonian Institute)

A Celebrated Industry

Figure 4.9 Kiln furniture from the Bradford Pottery in Kingston, Mass. A variety of other kiln artifacts were also recovered (courtesy Peter Follansbee)

Figure 4.10 Kiln furniture from the Bradford Pottery in Kingston, Mass. A variety of other kiln artifacts were also recovered (courtesy Peter Follansbee)

A Celebrated Industry

Figure 4.11a and 4.11b Kiln furniture from the Bradford Pottery in Kingston, Mass., as well as a stack of milk pans recovered at the site of the pottery. (courtesy Peter Follansbee)

Figure 4.12 Kiln saggars from the Bradford Pottery in Kingston, Mass. A variety of other kiln artifacts were also recovered (courtesy Peter Follansbee)

A Celebrated Industry

Figure 4.13 Kiln bricks from the Bradford Pottery in Kingston, Mass. A variety of kiln furniture and many other artifacts were also recovered (courtesy Peter Follansbee)

Figure 4.14 Kiln furniture from the Bradford Pottery in Kingston, Mass. A variety of other kiln artifacts were also recovered (courtesy Peter Follansbee)

A Celebrated Industry

Figure 4.15 Kiln furniture from the Bradford Pottery in Kingston, Mass. A variety of other kiln artifacts were also recovered (courtesy Peter Follansbee)

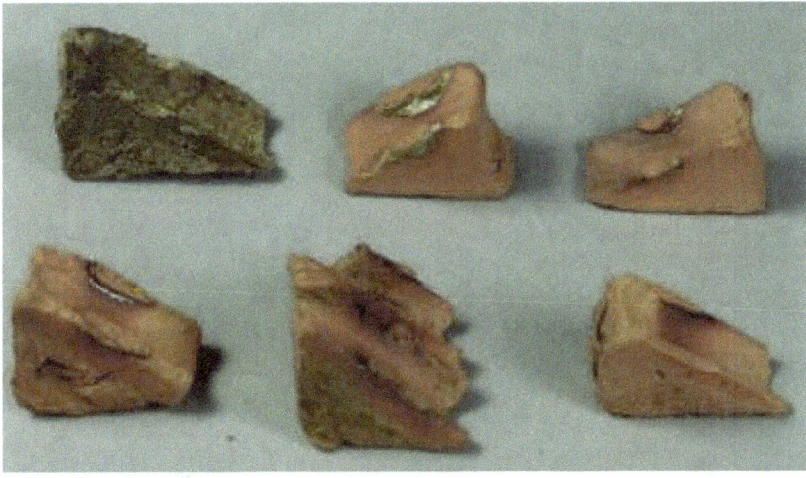

Figure 4.16 Kiln furniture from the Bradford Pottery in Kingston, Mass. A variety of other kiln artifacts were also recovered (courtesy Peter Follansbee)

A Celebrated Industry

Figure 4.17 Various cogglewheel decorated red earthenware sherds collected at the site of the Bradford Pottery in Kingston, Mass. (courtesy Peter Follansbee)

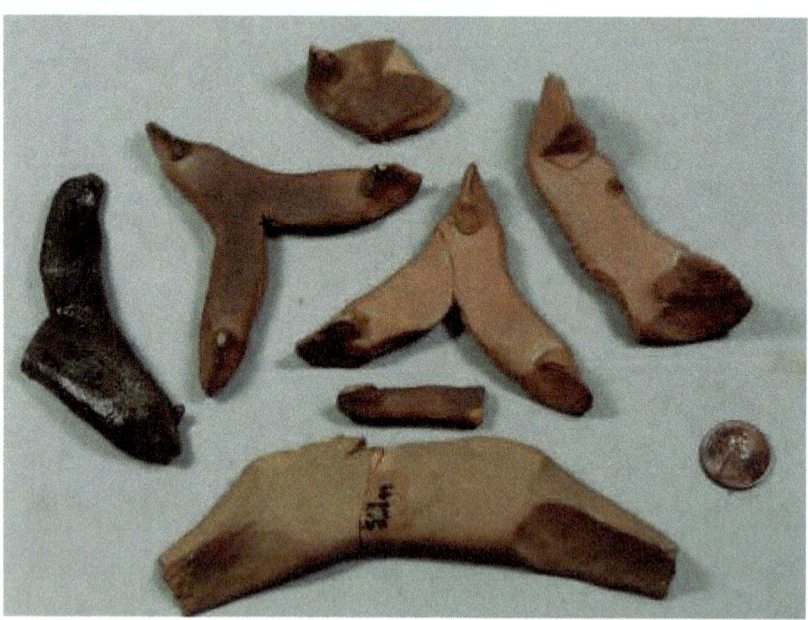

Figure 4.18 Kiln furniture from the Bradford Pottery in Kingston, Mass. A variety of other kiln artifacts were also recovered (courtesy Peter Follansbee)

A Celebrated Industry

Figure 4.19 Kiln furniture with some green glaze on it recovered from the site of the Stephen Bradford Pottery in Kingston, Mass. This image was also published in the 2017 issue of Ceramics in America. (courtesy Plimouth Plantation and the Jones River Village Historical Society)

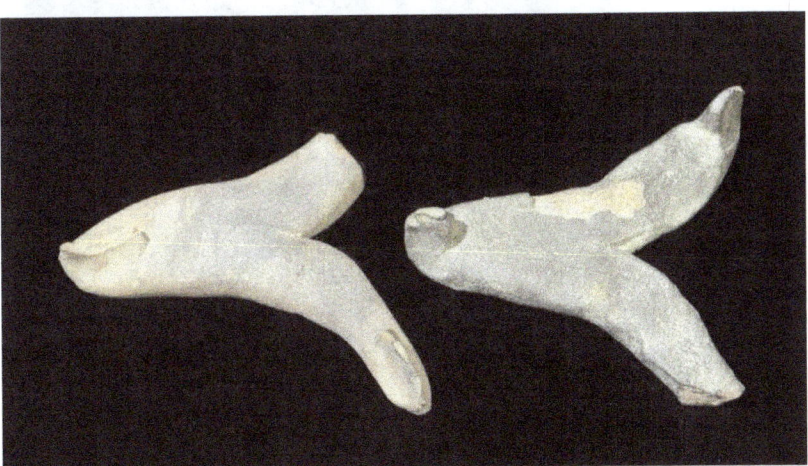

Figure 4.20 Kiln furniture recovered from the site of the Stephen Bradford Pottery in Kingston, Mass. This image was also published in the 2017 issue of Ceramics in America. (courtesy Plimouth Plantation and the Jones River Village Historical Society)

A Celebrated Industry

Figure 4.21 Red earthenware pitcher adorned with an exact cogglewheel decoration as a sherd recovered at the site of the Bradford Pottery in Kingston, Mass. by Lura Woodside Watkins. (courtesy National Museum of American History at the Smithsonian Institute)

Figure 4.22 Late eighteenth or early nineteenth century red earthenware pitchers thought to have been made in Kingston, Mass. based on archaeological evidence. They also sold in the Huntington Collection in Maine in 1974. (courtesy Dr. Brian Mills)

A Celebrated Industry

Figure 4.23 Late eighteenth or early nineteenth century red earthenware pitcher thought to have been made in Kingston, Mass. based on archaeological evidence. (courtesy Northeast Auctions)

Figure 4.24 Late eighteenth or early nineteenth century red earthenware pitcher thought to have been made in Kingston, Mass. based on archaeological evidence. (courtesy Skinner, previously owned by Charles D. Cook)

A Celebrated Industry

Figure 4.25 Late eighteenth or early nineteenth century red earthenware pitcher thought to have been made in Kingston, Mass. based on archaeological evidence. (courtesy John Sideli)

Figure 4.26 Late eighteenth or early nineteenth century red earthenware pitcher thought to have been made in Kingston, Mass. based on archaeological evidence. (courtesy Sam Herrup)

A Celebrated Industry

Figure 4.27 Red earthenware pot attributed to the Bradford Pottery in Kingston, Mass. based on the cogglewheel decoration and other characteristics. (courtesy Martha L. Sulya and the Kingston Public Library)

Figure 4.28a and 4.28b (Left) Red earthenware jar with a similar glaze when compared to some of the wares produced in Kingston. (Right) Red earthenware pot possibly attributed to the Bradford Pottery in Kingston, Mass. based on the cogglewheel decoration, which matches archaeological evidence. (courtesy Skinner, Lewis Scranton Collection)

A Celebrated Industry

Figure 4.29-4.30 These jars may have also been manufactured at the Bradford Pottery in Kingston, Mass. based on archaeological evidence (Inset photo of Figure 4.29) that seems to match this production in both the form of the jar and the glaze collected by Lura Woodside Watkins at the site of the pottery in 1945. (courtesy National Museum of American History at the Smithsonian Institute, Lewis Scranton and Sam Herrup)

A Celebrated Industry

Figure 4.31-4.32 Very similar if not the same style of decorated sherd recovered from a late eighteenth and early nineteenth century context at the site of the ca. 1721 Samuel Bell House in Salem, Mass.

Figure 4.33 The circa 1721 Samuel Bell House in Salem, Mass.

A Celebrated Industry

Figure 4.34 This pitcher is likely related to the jars illustrated in Figures 4.29 and 4.30. It sold as part of the Huntington Collection in Maine in 1974. (courtesy Crocker Farm)

A Celebrated Industry

Figure 4.35-4.36 This jar is attributed to the Bradford Pottery in Kingston, Mass. based on the cogglewheel decoration, which matches archaeological evidence recovered at the site of the pottery by Lura Woodside Watkin kept at the National Museum of American History at the Smithsonian Institute.

A Celebrated Industry

Figure 4.37 Late eighteenth or early nineteenth century red earthenware pitcher attributed to the Bradford Pottery in Kingston, Mass. based on the cogglewheel decoration below the rim. (courtesy Applebrook Auctions & Estate Sales)

Figure 4.38 Late eighteenth or early nineteenth century red earthenware pitcher attributed to the Bradford Pottery in Kingston, Mass. based on the cogglewheel decoration below the rim. (courtesy David Good)

A Celebrated Industry

Figure 4.39 This is the same pitcher that is illustrated in Figure 4.38. (courtesy New Haven Auctions)

Figure 4.40a and 4.40b (left) Red earthenware pitchers attributed to the Bradford Pottery in Kingston, Mass. The pitcher shown to the left was once owned by Ginsburg & Levy in the 1960s, a noted antiques shop in New York City. (courtesy James Julia and Freeman's Auction)

A Celebrated Industry

Figure 4.41 Red earthenware jar possibly related to wares manufactured by the Bradford family otherwise from another manufacturer in New England. (courtesy Ron & Penny Dionne Collection and Antiques Associates at West Townsend)

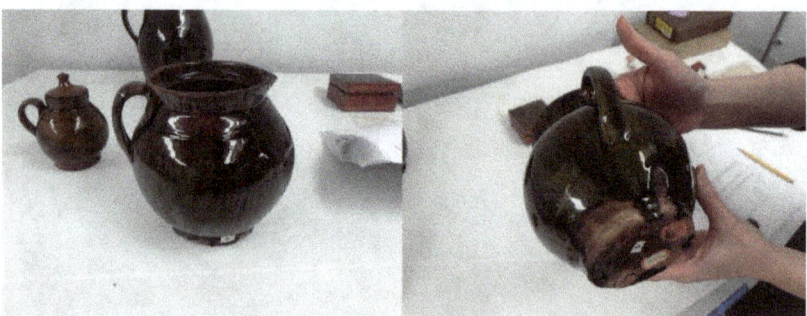

Figure 4.42 The manufacturer of this New England red earthenware pitcher shares some similarities with a known style of pitcher manufactured in Kingston, Mass., including the rim, the handle and the streaking black, brown and green glaze. (courtesy Albert Hastings Pitkin Collection, Wadsworth Atheneum)

A Celebrated Industry

Figure 4.43 Additional views of the pitcher illustrated to the right in Figure 4.22 (courtesy Jim and Janet Laverdiere)

Figure 4.44 Late eighteenth or early nineteenth century red earthenware pitcher attributed to the Bradford Pottery in Kingston, Mass. The rouletting matches archaeological evidence recovered at the site of the pottery and kept at both Plimouth Plantation and the National Museum of American History at the Smithsonian Institute. (courtesy Historic Deerrfield)

Figure 4.45 Late eighteenth or early nineteenth century red earthenware pitcher attributed to the Bradford Pottery in Kingston, Mass. From the collection of David Good. (Courtesy New Haven Auctions)

Figure 4.46 Late eighteenth or nineteenth century red earthenware cup; the form is similar to styles manufactured in northern New England, including Vermont, although the glaze is similar to some of the wares made in Kingston, Mass. Nonetheless, manufactured in New England. From the collection of David Good. (courtesy New Haven Auctions)

A Celebrated Industry

Bradford Archaeology at the Smithsonian Institute

Figure 4.47 Various red earthenware artifacts collected by Lura Woodside Watkins at the site of the Bradford Pottery in Kingston, Mass. in 1945. (courtesy National Museum of American History at the Smithsonian Institute in Washington, D.C.)

Figure 4.48 Various red earthenware artifacts collected by Lura Woodside Watkins at the site of the Bradford Pottery in Kingston, Mass. in 1945. (courtesy National Museum of American History at the Smithsonian Institute in Washington, D.C.)

A Celebrated Industry

Figure 4.49 and 4.50 Colorfully glazed sherd and kiln furniture recovered by Lura Woodside Watkins at the site of the Bradford Pottery in Kingston, Mass. in 1945. (courtesy National Museum of American History at the Smithsonian Institute in Washington, D.C.)

> Chapter 5

The Red Earthenware Industry in Bristol County, Mass.

The industry in Bristol County, Massachusetts was established decades before the American Revolution by Quakers intertwined with the potter's industry in South Danvers (today known as Peabody), Massachusetts. The most prominent businesses were operated by the Boyce and Shove families in Berkley, Massachusetts, and the Chace and Purinton families in Somerset, Massachusetts. Overall, there were dozens of potters involved with this industry, but there were also lesser-known individuals, which probably included apprentices and possibly traveling potters.

Similar to the businesses in Danvers/Peabody, where the industry was located near its major market in Salem, Massachusetts, the industry in Bristol County was strategically located near New Bedford, Massachusetts, and Rhode Island, utilizing the Taunton River and other avenues for transportation in order to distribute their wares. These were both major marketplaces before and after the American Revolution.

Interestingly, pottery production was such an important part of Somerset's early history that the central part of the town, where it was most prevalent was named Pottersville. Potters produced red earthenware in the Country Street and Riverside Avenues sections of town, all the way to the river. There are even some accounts that indicate at night, the glow from the potteries was a common scene.

A Celebrated Industry

The name Pottersville was a result of a plant created by Clark Chace Junior (1814-1881) and his brothers Benjamin and Leonard in 1840 when they built a stoneware plant. But the name is also indicative of the thriving red earthenware industry that had existed in Somerset prior to this period. A thriving stoneware industry also existed in Taunton, Massachusetts in the 1800s.

Figure 5.1 1887 map of "Pottersville" in Somerset, Mass.

Figure 5.2a-5.2b Circa 1885 stoneware butter crock attributed to the Somerset Potters Works, inscribed "Mrs. S.A. Eddy," and a stoneware urn with incised decoration highlighted with cobalt attributed to Somerset, Mass. (Courtesy Crocker Farm and Antiques Associates at West Townsend)

A Celebrated Industry

Figure 5.3 Circa 1850 stoneware pedestal base cooler stamped "Somerset / Potters Works." (Courtesy Crocker Farm)

Figure 5.4-5.5 Left) Circa 1880 six gallon stoneware crock attributed to the Somerset Potters Works; they incorporated various stenciled designs into production. Right) Circa 1850 stoneware pedestal base cooler stamped "Somerset / Potters Works." (Courtesy Crocker Farm and MV Auctions)

Figure 5.6 Circa 1850 stoneware pedestal base cooler stamped "Somerset / Potters Works / Somerset." (courtesy Colonial Williamsburg)

A Celebrated Industry

Figure 5.7 Nineteenth century cobalt decorated stoneware cooler made in the Taunton, Mass. area inscribed on the arms "Betsy Baker is my name" and "Taunton, Mass / July the 12 1834." (courtesy Crocker Farm)

Figure 5.8 Nineteenth century five gallon stoneware cooler inscribed "Shoot the first man who pulls down this flag / Gen Dix," stamped "F.T. Wright & Son / Taunton, MA." (courtesy Crocker Farm)

A Celebrated Industry

Some of the pottery that survives from this area today has been commonly called *"New Bedford"* due to the amount of Bristol County red earthenware that has been discovered in the city over the past 100 or more years.

Archaeology and the Little Compton, Rhode Island Historical Society have also proven that Rhode Island was a major export opportunity, especially during the circa 1780-1830 period. Archaeological evidence has been discovered throughout the state: For example, a few years ago, an archaeology dig at an eighteenth-century estate in Glocester, Rhode Island turned up at least five different glazed forms from Bristol County within a 1790-1820 archaeological context decorated with green, black, and orange glazes – and the Little Compton Historical Society (among other museums in Rhode Island) owns a variety of objects that retain local histories of ownership in Rhode Island.

Figure 5.9a Bristol County, Mass. red earthenware sherds recovered at an estate in Glocester, Rhode Island. (courtesy PAL Archaeology)

Figure 5.9b Nineteenth century red earthenware handled pot recovered at the North Shore archaeological site, which was the location of Providence, Rhode Island's Snowtown neighborhood of the 1820s to the 1840s. (courtesy PAL Archaeology)

Bristol County red earthenware sherds were also discovered in 2009 by archaeologists from the University of Massachusetts at Boston within a circa 1750-1820 archaeological context at the seventeenth century Waite-Kirby-Potter House in Westport, Massachusetts. Although, the most exciting example of ownership is perhaps green glazed sherds that are likely from this industry that were recovered by archaeologists in 2006 within a pre-1840 context at the site of the nineteenth century African American Meeting House in Boston.

According to National Park Service, *"The African-American Meeting House on Beacon Hill in Boston was built in 1806 in what was once the heart of Boston's free black community. The Meeting House was host to giants in the Abolitionist Movement who were responsible for monumental historical events that changed this nation."* The sherds were recovered within such a context that they may have belonged to the site when the meeting house was used to *"found the New England Anti-Slavery Society with William Lloyd Garrison (1805-1879) in 1832 and the 1833 farewell address of Maria Stewart (1803-1879), a black woman and the first American born woman to speak publicly before a gender mixed audience."*

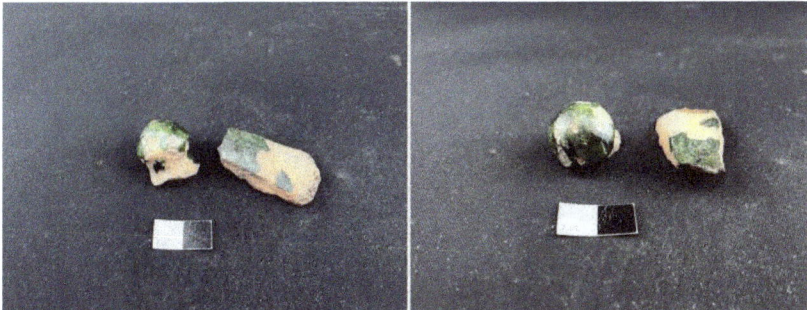

Figure 5.10 Green glazed red earthenware sherds from a lid likely made in Bristol County, Mass. recovered at the site of the African American Meeting House in Boston. (courtesy City of Boston Archaeology Department)

Sherds resembling glazes produced in Bristol County have also been recovered in Providence, Rhode Island and possibly Manhattan in New York City, among other locations.

A Celebrated Industry

The sherds recovered in Providence were found on the site of the John Brown House. According to the Rhode Island Historical Society, *"The John Brown House was built in 1788 by merchant, patriot, politician and unfortunately slave trader John Brown (1736-1803), who was also an instigator and participant in the Gaspee Affair, a conflict between American patriots and British soldiers that took place in Narragansett Bay in 1772. Brown and his family were some of the wealthiest and most influential people in the colonies, and then the United States. The Browns are also the namesake of Brown University in Providence."*

Figure 5.11a (Left) Green glazed sherd recovered in Manhattan; glaze is similar to those manufactured in Bristol County, Mass., although the origin of this artifact is unknown. (Right) Green glaze sherd recovered at the John Brown House in Providence, Rhode Island. (courtesy Adam Woodward and Brown University Archaeology Department)

Figure 5.12 Green glazed red earthenware sherd recovered at the site of the Industrial School for Girls in Dorchester, Mass. Due to the late 1800s context this is noteworthy, but not from Bristol County, Mass. (courtesy City of Boston Archaeology Program)

A Celebrated Industry

Among the eighteenth-century documents in existence today is a 1792 ship manifest for the sloop Defiance traveling from Dighton, Massachusetts to New York City, signed by master James Nichols (d. 1811) of Berkely, Massachusetts, who was also a Captain in the American Revolution. Aboard the ship was Simeon Bush (1763-1836) and the household furniture for three people who were traveling with him, as well as seven different items being shipped by Nichols. Those items include *"hollow ware, nails, buttons, hats, earthen ware and cloth."* It is likely that the *"earthen ware"* was manufactured locally in Bristol County, and it may not be a coincidence either that the sherd recovered in Manhattan that is illustrated in Figure 5.11a resembles wares produced in Bristol County. A docket indicates that the sloop arrived in New York on June 4, 1792.

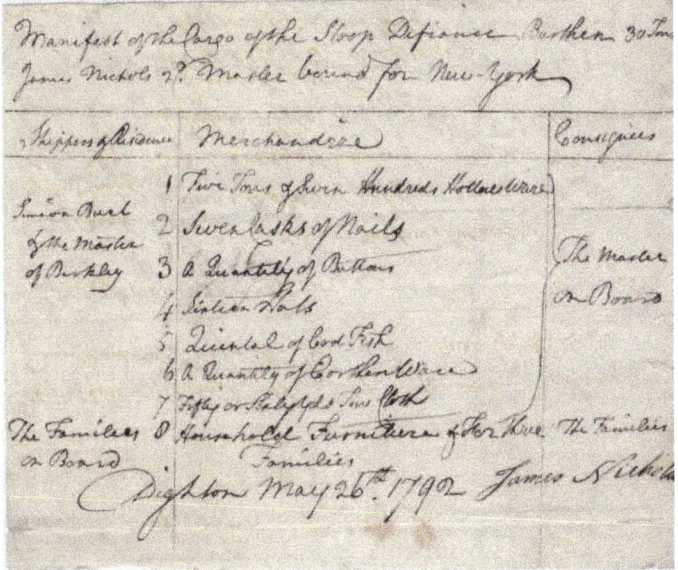

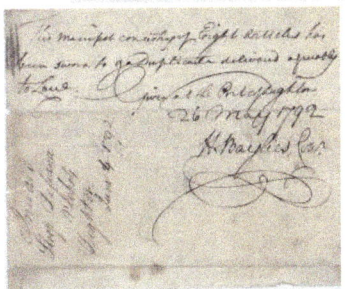

Figure 5.11b Document from 1792 that reveals various items aboard the ship Defiance being shipped from Massachusetts to New York City. Among those items is a selection of "earthen ware." (courtesy private collection)

A Celebrated Industry

Interestingly, among the surviving Bristol County objects known to exist today retaining an early history of ownership are two jars that were reportedly owned by the Nye family (see also Figures 8.29-8.30) on Nantucket, which was also a prominent family on Cape Cod. Both Nantucket and Cape Cod were among the places that Bristol County pottery was sold.

Figure 5.13 Late eighteenth or early nineteenth century red earthenware jars attributed to Bristol County, Mass., reportedly retaining a history of ownership with the Nye family on Nantucket.

However, the potters were not the only persons responsible for peddling the wares from this industry. Winterthur's library in Delaware owns a circa 1757-1766 account book kept by Preserved Peirce (1736-1798), a merchant from Swansea, Massachusetts, who traded along the coast of Rhode Island and Connecticut. He bartered with wooden and pewter goods, pottery and tools for

Figure 5.14 Preserved Peirce's 1757-1766 account book. (courtesy Winterthur)

craftsmen and potters. The book reveals that he purchased red earthenware from potters John Law, Caleb Purinton, and Isaac Upton.

Issac and his brother, Samuel Upton were potters likely employed in Berkley in the 1760s, when they interacted with Peirce, although, they later went on to build a business in East Greenwich, Rhode Island, circa 1771-1783 that they have garnered some fame for today. Unfortunately, some of the early-published articles have attributed a number of objects to the business in East Greenwich, many of which are green glazed, and as a result of where those objects were found in Rhode Island. But by what is known today most of these objects are actually from the eighteenth and early nineteenth century red earthenware industry in Bristol County.

Massachusetts author Lura Woodside Watkins also cites a post-American Revolution account book from Peirce that she previously owned now in the Smithsonian, when she published *Early New England Potters and Their Wares* in 1950. *"Preserved Peirce owned a sloop called Rosemary, in which he sailed up and down Mount Hope Bay and along the coast of Rhode Island and Connecticut selling wooden ware, pewter, pottery, and such articles as tea kettles, hats, and shoe buckles, or bartering his stock for flour or flax, lead and manganese for the potters, or brass and metal for copperworkers."*

The book verifies that Peirce was still in business with the Purinton family, much like he was before the American Revolution, but he was also in business with the Shove family. An entry from 1786 reveals the red earthenware forms that Peirce had in his possession included milk pans, platters, plates, basins, pots, bread pans, chamber pots, jugs, pitchers, mugs, bowls, porringers, and churns.

Another important daybook is one owned by the Baker Library at Harvard University kept by George Shove (b. 1738) in Dighton, Massachusetts from 1768-1810. The book records the sales of his wares and general merchandise. The items sold include red earthenware jugs, plates, bowls, cups, and chamber pots, as well as shoes, indigo, beaver hats, sheep's wool, farm produce and wholesale brick. Payment was made in cash and

A Celebrated Industry

services including blacksmithing, tailoring, and spinning, and hoops, lumber, meat, sugar, molasses rice and rum. One of his frequent customers was Adonijah Upton, a glazier in Dighton; additional names include Elizabeth Hathaway of Freetown, Massachusetts, Daniel Smith of Newport, Rhode Island, and Nantucket whaler William Rotch Senior (1734-1828). A number of accounts dated 1785-1791 reference the sloop Friendship, which voyaged from Newport to North Carolina carrying Shove's wares; and his shared expenses related to the ship with Lydia Boyes. For instance, in 1776, he charged Boyes for sundry vessels of ware for spinners. She may have been a business partner of Shove, and he probably also operated a general store.

There is no indication in this book that this George Shove was a potter, although another George Shove who was a potter did work in neighboring Berkley. The Shove from Dighton was unquestionably related and if he was not a potter himself, then he was most likely selling wares perhaps made by his family and possibly even other Bristol County potters. There was a lot of trade that happened with the Quakers, especially when it came to utilitarian pottery in this part of New England.

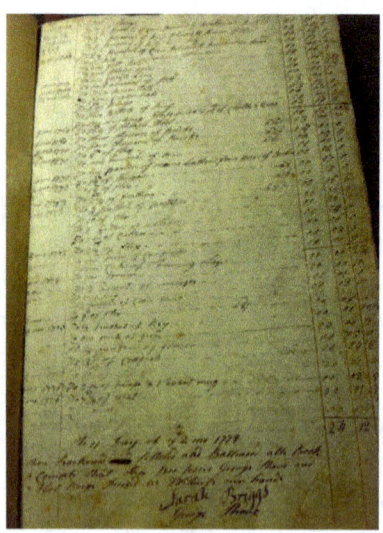

Figure 5.15 A page from George Shove's pottery daybook from 1768-1810 that he kept in Dighton, Mass. His name is signed at the bottom. (courtesy Baker Library, Harvard University)

A Celebrated Industry

Figure 5.16 Excellent formed Bristol County, Mass. jar that is similar in shape to Chinese ginger jars.

The most famous of the forms made in this industry today are certainly the colorful lidded ovoid jars from the late eighteenth and early nineteenth century, which in some ways resemble porcelain ginger jars made in China for centuries. The jars are sometimes inscribed on the base with a number, letter or a Roman numeral that usually matches an inscription also found on the lid. This industry is also distinguished today for its vibrant green glazes, which certainly may have garnered these potters some recognition for when these objects were originally created.

Figure 5.17 Bristol County, Mass. jars with inscribed bases; left to right: Roman numeral "XI" or "IX," the letter "C" and the number "5."

The industry in Bristol County must even held some kind of influence with craftsmen located elsewhere in New England. As it may be that influence or similarities seem apparent with some wares made by Peter Clark, John Henry Benner and the Bradford family in Kingston and Cape Cod. This industry is also responsible for training Elijah Cornell II, who later went on to establish an important pottery in upstate New York, and his son, Ezra Cornell, also a potter, founded Cornell University in 1865.

It is difficult to properly attribute red earthenware from Bristol County to a single potter today much like it is with the colonial potter's industry in Charlestown, Massachusetts and the eighteenth and nineteenth century production that occurred in Danvers/Peabody. There were just so many family businesses that produced similar products with overlap from potters who worked at multiple companies. Although, there are some marriage jars and possible presentation pieces that survive today that can be associated with a specific family.

The industry in Bristol County Massachusetts is one of the few locations in New England known to have manufactured red earthenware marriage jars in the nineteenth century. For instance, a pair of marriage jars are displayed at the Metropolitan Museum of Art in Manhattan that were made for George and Debby Purinton at the Purinton Pottery in Somerset in 1809. The names adorn each jar in slip along with birds and other decorative features. A rundlet is also known with a very similar bird decorated in slip on either end that is thought to be related.

Figure 5.18-5.19 (Top) Red earthenware marriage jars made in 1809 at the Purinton Pottery in Somerset, Mass. for George and Debby Purinton. The jars are heavily decorated in slip, including birds. (Bottom) A red earthenware rundlet manufactured in Bristol County with a similar bird applied in slip on each end. (courtesy Metropolitan Museum of Art and Crocker Farm)

A Celebrated Industry

There are also other jars known that are believed to have been made by the Purinton family. One of those jars is dated under one handle in slip, "*1812*" and the initials, "*A.P.*" are found under the other handle in slip. The jar may have been made for an important event, such as a wedding, and it is decorated with a bright orange glaze, splashes of bright green glaze and a floral decoration in slip.

Figure 5.20 Early nineteenth century slip decorated red earthenware marriage or presentation jar from Bristol County, Mass. dated under one handle "1812" and the initials "AP" are found under the other handle. (courtesy Hilary & Paulette Nolan Collection)

Otherwise, it has proven difficult to identify what exactly was made where and by whom with the little archaeology that survives from this industry today. However, Watkins did donate a colorfully glazed sherd to the National Museum of American History at the Smithsonian Institute in Washington, D.C. in the twentieth century. She recovered the green and plum colored sherd with a crimped rim in Somerset, which suggests that it was made by either the Chace or Purinton families. The glaze on the sherd also closely resembles a sherd recovered at the estate in Glocester, Rhode Island, which is similar to the colors found on a surviving pitcher, as well as a few other known objects.

A Celebrated Industry

Figure 5.21 (Right) Unusual plum and green glazed sherd recovered by Lura Woodside Watkins in Somerset, Mass., together with a (Left) matching glazed red earthenware pitcher from Bristol County, likely made in Somerset. (courtesy National Museum of American History at the Smithsonian Institute)

The variety of forms made in Bristol County was as diverse as any industry in New England in the eighteenth or nineteenth century. Aside from the ovoid jars that came in a variety of sizes, there also appears to have been an emphasis given to rundlets for carrying liquid, which is unusual when compared to what was produced elsewhere in New England during the period. But there was also a large focus given to the production of jars, jugs and pitchers that are known in a variety of shapes, glazes, and sizes today. The production of pans and plates with white or green slip was also fashionable, but this is a style of production that may have been more prominent in the 1700s rather than the 1800s, and it is sometimes difficult to differentiate these pieces to similar wares made around the same period in West Hartford, Connecticut (Figure 5.41). The scarce forms to see today include bottles, possibly bird bottles, bowls, flasks, harvest jugs, inkwells, sanders, along with teacups and saucers.

Much like the other industries in coastal Massachusetts, the industry in Bristol County achieved its own identity in the eighteenth and nineteenth century. Its existence is characterized today by the skill, creativity, variety, and color that this industry produced. It was because of this production that in essence it was by itself from what was produced elsewhere in New England during the period.

A Celebrated Industry

Figure 5.22-5.23 Slip decorated red earthenware sherds and other red earthenware artifacts, along with kiln furniture recovered from the Shove/Osborn Pottery site in Berkley, Mass. by Andrea Pontes. Published in Brian Cullity's 1991 exhibit catalog Slipped and Glazed: Regional American Redware. The small creamer or pitcher to the right and some of the artifacts that surround it may not be locally made.

A Celebrated Industry

I can only begin to imagine how these types of wares were originally received in the general marketplace. Production must have been anticipated for wherever these objects were eventually sold. Although, the aesthetic and artistic merit is what has attracted collectors and museums for at a least a century now, where that same brilliance must have been recognized by the homeowners, who originally owned these types of products for their utilitarian needs in the 1700s and 1800s.

One form sometimes associated with the Bristol County industry of particular interest is a straight sided jar that is known in multiple sizes and a variety of glazes. The production and clay color of this form is unlike most everything else associated with production in Bristol County, although, it is likely related to a style of pitcher (Figures 5.25 and 5.28) from the southeastern Massachusetts region (unlikely Rhode Island) and a jar with the same type of handles (Figure 5.31). Without more evidence, it is unknown if this type of straight sided jar was made in Bristol County or elsewhere in southeastern Massachusetts. It should be noted though that this form is also illustrated in picture 50 in *Early New England Potters and Their* as probably being from Connecticut, but it was not manufactured there and probably instead found in Connecticut (Figure 5.24)

Figure 5.24 Nineteenth century red earthenware jar manufactured in southeastern Mass. or Bristol County, Mass., which is illustrated in picture 50 in Early New England Potters and Their Wares. This form has previously been attributed to Bristol County, but more evidence is probably needed to make that attribution, even though the glaze and rounded foot on this particular jar is similar to Bristol County production. (courtesy National Museum of American History at the Smithsonian Institute)

A Celebrated Industry

Figure 5.25 Both of these pieces are most likely related – they share a number of production characteristics that seem to be from the same area or business.

Figure 5.26 Left) Nineteenth century green glazed red earthenware jar most likely manufactured in southeastern Mass. (courtesy Garth's Auctions)

Figure 5.27 Left) Nineteenth century green glazed red earthenware jar most likely manufactured in southeastern Mass. (courtesy Northeast Auctions)

A Celebrated Industry

Figure 5.28 Another look at the jar and pitcher illustrated in Figure 5.25.

Figure 5.29-5.30 There are also similarities found in this style of straight sided jar when compared to this large early ovoid jar; the similarities include the manufacture of the handles and the rim, but it is unclear if there is any direct relationship.

A Celebrated Industry

Figure 5.31 Late eighteenth or early nineteenth century green glazed red earthenware jar attributed to southeastern Mass., possibly from Bristol County and most likely related to the jar and pitcher illustrated in Figures 5.25 and 5.28. The handles on this jar are the same or very similar to those illustrated on the straight sided jar shown in those figures. (courtesy Private Collection)

Figure 5.32 Two outstanding glazed late eighteenth or early nineteenth century red earthenware jars attributed to Bristol County, Mass.

A Celebrated Industry

Figure 5.33 Late eighteenth or early nineteenth century green glazed red earthenware jar probably related to those discusses in Figures 5.25, 5.28 and 5.31. The jar is manufactured with a number of similar characteristics, including the two exterior handles. (courtesy Historic Deerfield)

A Celebrated Industry

Figure 5.34 Two extremely rare decorated late eighteenth or early nineteenth century objects attributed to Bristol County, Mass. (courtesy Pook & Pook Inc.)

Figure 5.35 Late eighteenth or early nineteenth century green glazed red earthenware pitcher attributed to Bristol County, Mass. A similar pitcher is in the collection of The Bennington Museum in Vermont.

A Celebrated Industry

Figure 5.36 Some outstanding green glazes from Bristol County, Mass.

Figure 5.37 Two outstanding pitchers; the pitcher to the left is most likely from Bristol County, although there is an old note accompanying a related piece in the collection of Historic Deerfield that says it was made on Cape Cod (see Chapter 7). The pitcher to the right is highly unusual where the base is a jar that has been converted into a pitcher; this type of transformation is more common with early glass.

A Celebrated Industry

Figure 5.38 Two matching formed jars with different glazes from either southeastern Massachusetts or Bristol County, Mass.

Figure 5.39 Various jars from Bristol County, Mass. with different glazes.

A Celebrated Industry

Figure 5.40a Late eighteenth or early nineteenth century red earthenware jar attributed to Bristol County, Mass. The lid and jar are both inscribed with the same letter "A" and the lid is also embellished with a Quaker style hat finial. The jar may have been made for a relative of an unidentified Bristol County potter perhaps to honor their Quaker heritage or it may have been made for another related reason. See Figure 40b for additional information. (courtesy Sam Herrup)

A Celebrated Industry

Figure 5.40b Portraits of Moses Brown (1738-1836), a famed Quaker from Rhode Island, who was an abolitionist and industrialist. The Quaker hat that he is wearing is very similar to that adorning the lid in Figure 5.40a. (courtesy Brown University)

A Celebrated Industry

Figure 5.41 Left) Late eighteenth or early nineteenth century slip decorated red earthenware dish attributed to the Hartford, Connecticut area, probably from West Hartford; Right) Late eighteenth or early nineteenth century slip decorated red earthenware dish attributed to Bristol County, Mass. The East Greenwich, Rhode Island Historical Society happens to own a number of dishes related to this example.

Figure 5.42 Late eighteenth or early nineteenth century red earthenware rundlet similar to those often attributed to Bristol County, Mass., although this example was purportedly manufactured at the Joseph Dodge (1776-1849) Pottery in Portsmouth, N.H. (courtesy Yale University Art Gallery)

A Celebrated Industry

Figure 5.43 Artwork of a jar with a cover probably from Bristol County, Mass. done by Alfred Parys for the Index of American Design in 1939. (courtesy National Gallery of Art at the Smithsonian Institute)

A Celebrated Industry

Figure 5.44 Artwork of a green glazed jug from Bristol County, Mass. done by John Matulis (1910-2000) for the Index of American Design in 1936. (courtesy National Gallery of Art at the Smithsonian Institute)

Figure 5.45a Nineteenth century black glazed red earthenware jug probably made in Bristol County, Mass. "Bk PERU 1853" is painted on the jug with an old hemp cordage harness. "Loaned by Frank Wood" is written on the base; Wood was appointed curator of the New Bedford Whaling Museum in 1914. It is probably safe to say that some Bristol County red earthenware found its way onto ships in New Bedford's harbor in the eighteenth and nineteenth century. (courtesy New Bedford Whaling Museum)

Figure 5.45b View of New Bedford Harbor From the Fort Near Fairhaven, 1845, Fitz Henry Lane (1804-1865). (courtesy New Bedford Whaling Museum)

A Celebrated Industry

Figure 5.46-5.47 Charles E. Hathaway (1853-1944) was the last of the old professional potters of Somerset, Mass., retiring at the close of World War I. In 1940 he came out of retirement during Somerset's sesquicentennial celebration, and, using his old wheel, demonstrated he had lost none of his skill. His wheel is owned by the Somerset Historical Society today, which also owns a selection of locally made pottery. Below is a list of Somerset's potters. (courtesy Somerset Historical Society)

HONOR ROLL OF THE SOMERSET POTTERS

BROWN, GEORGE
CHACE, ASA
CHACE, BENJAMIN C.
CHACE, BENJAMIN G.
CHACE, CLARK
CHACE, CLARK
CHACE, ENOCH B.
CHACE, JOSEPH
CHACE, LEONARD
CHACE, LLOYD
CHACE, STEPHEN
CHACE, STEPHEN II
CHACE, STEPHEN III
CLEVELAND, BENJAMIN
COLLINS, SAMUEL B.

CORNELL, ELIJAH
GRAY, JOSEPH
HATHAWAY, CHAS. E.
KENNEY, THOMAS
PURINTON, CLARK
PURINTON, CLARK JR.
PURINTON, GEORGE
PURINGTON, DAVID
PURINGTON, DEXTER
PURINGTON, GEORGE S.
PURINGTON, SAMUEL
SHOVE, NATHANIEL
SHOVE, THEOPHILUS JR.
SYNAN, PATRICK
SYNAN, WILLIAM

A Celebrated Industry

Old Colony Historical Museum in Taunton, Mass.

Figure 5.48a and 5.48b Late eighteenth or early nineteenth century red earthenware bowl thought to have been made in either Swansea or Taunton in Bristol County, Mass. (courtesy Old Colony History Museum in Taunton, Mass. and Rick Hamelin)

Figure 5.49 Nineteenth century American red earthenware jar that originally belonged to Cora Johnson Briggs of Taunton, circa 1800-1860. (courtesy Old Colony History Museum in Taunton, Mass.)

A Celebrated Industry

Figure 5.50 Early nineteenth century red earthenware pot used by Mrs. Mercy (Gilbert) Francis (b. August 25, 1776) of Taunton. (courtesy Old Colony History Museum in Taunton, Mass.)

Figure 5.51 Nineteenth century red earthenware milk pan used in Berkley, Mass. by the Macomber-Winslow family. (courtesy Old Colony History Museum in Taunton, Mass.)

Figure 5.52 Circa 1875 red earthenware pan stamped "F.T. Wright & Son / Stone Ware / Taunton, Mass." There are a small group of these pans known to exist today. (courtesy Crocker Farm Auctions of American Redware and Stoneware)

A Celebrated Industry

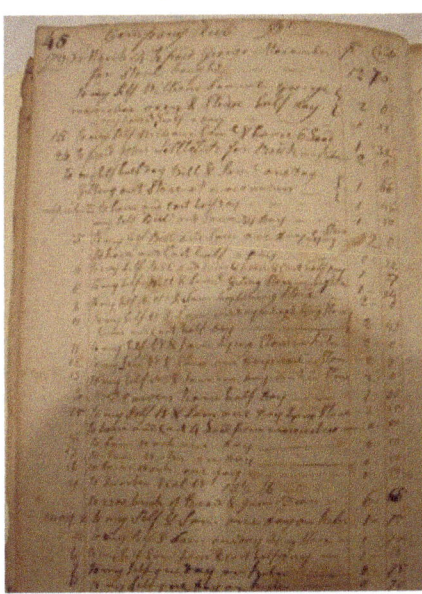

Figure 5.53 and 5.54 A page from William Seaver's (1743-1815) account book, a circa 1772-1815 red earthenware and stoneware potter in Taunton, Mass. According to Massachusetts potter Rick Hamelin's research, "Seaver began his career as a potter at Nathaniel Baker's business in Dorchester, Mass., although he eventually relocated to Taunton, where he obtained his stoneware clay from Martha's Vineyard and New Jersey." Taunton may not be as well known as some of the other Bristol County pottery centers, but there were also a number of potters located here in the 1700s and 1800s. (courtesy Old Colony History Museum in Taunton, Mass.)

A Celebrated Industry

> Chapter 6

Elijiah Cornell's Pottery Production

Founded in Ithaca, New York in 1865, Cornell University is among America's elite colleges, although it may not be widely known that the school is named after one of its founders, Ezra Cornell (1807-1874) who was the son of an accomplished red earthenware and stoneware potter.

Figure 6.1 This is Elijiah Cornell II (1771-1862)

Born in Swansea, Massachusetts, Elijah Cornell II (1771-1862) was the second son of Elijah (ca. 1730-1777) and Sarah (Miller) Cornell (1746-1774), who were farmers and devout Puritans. The family belonged to the Society of Friends; a group dedicated to the Quaker religion. At the age of nineteen, Elijah signed a contract, dated January 28, 1791, agreeing to apprentice at Asa Chase's (1744-1812) Pottery in Somerset, Bristol County, Massachusetts. Asa and Elijah were related by marriage. Bristol County and the collective industry in southeastern Massachusetts and Cape Cod is known for its skill, forms, glazes and some slipware, types of production that ultimately must have influenced the wares Cornell made later in his life. Quaker potters also drove much of this industry.

On July 4, 1805, Elijah married Eunice Barnard (1788-1857), having eleven children in their lifetime, six sons and five daughters, all of whom lived to see adulthood. Eunice came from

156

A Celebrated Industry

Figure 6.2 This is Ezra Cornell (1807-1874)

a family of seamen, artisans, and farmers. Their first child, Ezra was born in Westchester Landing in New York City on January 11, 1807; his birthplace is found today at 1515 Williamsbridge Road in the Bronx (Figure 6.3-6.4).

Census records indicate that Elijah was living in Westchester Landing, circa 1805-1808 and circa 1811-1814. He may have been employed in the pottery industry during his first tenure, but he is known to have worked in the shipping industry as a carpenter and lost money in a ship venture. Although, the family moved to De Ruyter, Madison County, New York, when they purchased 150 acres of land for $375. Around 1810, the Cornells returned to Westchester Landing, where Elijah found work as a supervisor in a pottery. It was published by Susan Lang in the Cornell Chronicle in 2007: *"The War of 1812 halted imports of English pottery, increasing the demand for local cheap, brown earthenware. Elijah had also worked at the Queens Ware Pottery in West Farms (west-central Bronx), where he learned to produce high-grade white ware. But at war's end, the market was flooded with cheaper English ware.*

Once again, Elijah moved with his family, this time to seek better markets in New Jersey. And as he had done from the age of six, Ezra helped in his father's business, running errands and, later, serving as a traveling salesman."

The Cornells moved to Bergen County, New Jersey, where Elijah may have had some exposure to a red earthenware pottery established about 1811 by Henry Jacob Van Saun (d. 1829) in River Edge, located about sixteen miles north of Manhattan. The known wares produced in River Edge include a variety of slipware, although, the family eventually settled in De Ruyter in 1819, where they farmed and established a red earthenware business.

Figure 6.3 My niece Alexis and I at the birthplace of Ezra Cornell at 1515 Williamsbridge Road in the Bronx in New York City.

Figure 6.4 The birthplace of Ezra Cornell at 1515 Williamsbridge Road in the Bronx in New York City. A McDonald's is located there today.

A Celebrated Industry

Figure 6.5 Nineteenth century slip decorated red earthenware dish probably made in River Edge, Bergen County, N.J., recovered in Paterson, N.J., which is about eight miles northwest of Manhattan.

Figure 6.6 (Left) Red earthenware plate manufactured by Henry Jacob Van Saun in River Edge, New Jersey commemorating Marquis de Lafayette's (1757-1834) visit to America in the 1820s. (Right) Also a commemorative plate manufactured by Van Saun painted for the Index of American Design by Yolande Delasser in 1937. (courtesy National Gallery of Art at the Smithsonian Institute)

A Celebrated Industry

Ezra helped his father build the pottery, but he left the family home in the spring of 1826, finding his way to Syracuse, New York as a journeyman carpenter. Afterwards, he moved to Homer, New York, where he was employed in a machine shop, and later Ithaca in 1828, eventually becoming a state senator, president of the State's Agricultural Society, and amassing a fortune in the telegraph business, connecting lines from Philadelphia, New York City, Albany, and parts of the Midwest. His involvement with politics led to his concern in higher education, and so he established Cornell University on April 27, 1865, on his farm in Ithaca, where he contributed the initial $500,000 endowment. The family also continued to serve in New York's political system under Ezra's son, Alonzo Cornell (1832-1904) who served as the state's twenty-seventh governor from 1880-1882.

Figure 6.7 The Cornell house in De Ruyter, New York. (courtesy Cornell University)

The history of the Cornell Pottery would be largely forgotten today if it were not for Massachusetts author Lura Woodside Watkins (1897-1982), who visited the location of the Cornell Pottery before she published *Early New England Potters and*

A Celebrated Industry

Their Wares in 1950. *"In 1943, we visited this site and were rewarded by the discovery of a small collection of fragments. Elijah had evidently advanced somewhat beyond the rather restrained technique of the Massachusetts potters, for in De Ruyter he decorated a good deal of his ware with slip of two colors, black and white, either marbled or applied in bold wavy (and straight) lines against backgrounds of contrasting hue."*

While studying these artifacts now in the collection of the National Museum of American History at the Smithsonian Institute in Washington, D.C., I considered the fact that some of the slip decorated sherds resemble a style of decoration found on a known large upstate New York red earthenware jar. New York archaeologist and museum specialist, George R. Hamell who is responsible for a lot of the published material and archaeology from red earthenware potters based in central and western New York State, had previously owned the jar. There is a small group of these jars known to exist today, where some are even glazed green. It appears that these jars were made in two-halves before they were joined together.

Figure 6.8 Slip decorated red earthenware jar from the collection of New York archaeologist and museum specialist, George R. Hamell. The style of the slip and the colors are similar to the artifacts collected by Lura Woodside Watkins at the site of the Cornell Pottery in De Ruyter, New York. (courtesy Crocker Farm)

A Celebrated Industry

Even so, there is not a lot of information known about the wares made at the Cornell Pottery; Elijah was clearly an accomplished potter, but this was not likely a fulltime job. He was a farmer, and the pottery business was probably used as a way to supplement the family's yearly income. It is difficult to say how often his kiln was fired; nevertheless, some American potter/farmers fired their kiln as little as once a year, while others fired it more frequently.

In the collection of Cornell University are some examples of Elijah's production, such as an unglazed flowerpot with an attached saucer and an unglazed vase. The University's collection also includes a brightly glazed pitcher that is somewhat similar in form to pitchers made in western New York during the same period. But the color of the glaze is of particular interest seeing that it closely resembles one of the more popular glazes manufactured by the Gleason family in Morganville, New York, about the mid-1800s.

The Cornell Pottery apparently operated in De Ruyter until about 1840, when it is noted by Ezra's biographer, Philip Dorf (1901-1981) who published *The Builder: A Biography of Ezra Cornell* in 1952, that, *"In the summer of 1842, in his 71st year, Father Elijah burned his first kiln of Ithaca ware."* Apparently, with the help of his sons, Elijah built a small kiln in Ithaca in 1842, where successive owners made stoneware until about 1890. The site was excavated in 1975 by archaeologists and students from Cornell University, including Dr. Carol Griggs, recovering a wide variety of artifacts, such as kiln furniture and sherds stamped with various maker marks. Elijah continued to work in Ithaca until at least 1850, where he is listed as a seventy-eight-year-old potter in the 1850 United States Federal Census. Among the notable potters who worked at the Cornell Pottery was Justus Morton (1801-1859), circa 1842-1844.

However, the 1860 United States Federal Census lists Elijah as an eighty-eight-year-old potter in Albion, Calhoun County, Michigan. He had migrated to Michigan because his son Ezra established the Michigan Telegraph Company in Albion in 1846. This production is unknown today; the wares he may have produced here were probably similar to those made in upstate

A Celebrated Industry

New York. But only a few years after he arrived, Elijah died in 1862, being buried in Riverside Cemetery in Albion. His wife, Eunice was buried alongside him when she passed away in 1874.

Interestingly, Cornell University is not the only prestigious American college or university named after clay workers. Tufts University in Medford, Massachusetts was established from land donated by Charles Tufts (1781-1876), who accrued his wealth from a brickmaking factory he owned in Medford. In fact, the Tufts name is synonymous with Medford's Colonial brick industry, and somewhat intertwined with the pottery industry in Charlestown, Massachusetts. The Tufts were descendants of Peter Tufts (1617-1700), an early Colonist who migrated to America from England around 1637.

Figure 6.9 Red earthenware pitcher attributed to Elijah Cornell in De Ruyter, New York, circa 1820-1840. The glaze is similar to a popular glaze produced by the Gleason family in Morganville, New York. The flowerpot and vase are also attributed to the Cornell Pottery. (courtesy Cornell University)

Figure 6.10 Nineteenth century stoneware made in Ithaca, New York; both marked "Ithaca." (courtesy Ted Sobel)

A Celebrated Industry

Figure 6.11-6.12 Some of the slip decorated red earthenware sherds recovered in 1943 by Lura Woodside Watkins at the site of the Cornell Pottery in De Ruyter, New York. (courtesy National Museum of American History at the Smithsonian Institute)

A Celebrated Industry

Figure 6.13-6.14 Some of the slip decorated red earthenware sherds recovered in 1943 by Lura Woodside Watkins at the site of the Cornell Pottery in De Ruyter, New York. (courtesy National Museum of American History at the Smithsonian Institute)

A Celebrated Industry

Figure 6.15a Two jars that match the production of the jar owned by George R. Hamell. The green glazed jar was found in central Pennsylvania, while the other jar was found in a thrift shop in Los Angeles.

Figure 6.15b Moments after my nephew Jason and I discovered the green glazed jar in central Pennsylvania, also illustrated in Figure 6.15a.

A Celebrated Industry

Figure 6.16 Related nineteenth century red earthenware jar as others discussed in this chapter, discovered in southern Alabama, stands 12 ½" tall. (courtesy David Richardson)

Figure 6.17 Related nineteenth century slip decorated red earthenware jar as others discussed in this chapter, stands 15" tall. (courtesy Crocker Farm Auctions of American Redware and Stoneware)

A Celebrated Industry

Cornell Archaeology at the Smithsonian Institute

Figure 6.18 Various types of slip-decorated red earthenware artifacts recovered by Lura Woodside Watkins at the site of the Cornell Pottery in De Ruyter, New York in 1945. (courtesy National Museum of American History at the Smithsonian Institute)

Figure 6.19 Various types of red earthenware artifacts recovered by Lura Woodside Watkins at the site of the Cornell Pottery in De Ruyter, New York in 1945. (courtesy National Museum of American History at the Smithsonian Institute)

A Celebrated Industry

Figure 6.20 Various types of red earthenware artifacts recovered by Lura Woodside Watkins at the site of the Cornell Pottery in De Ruyter, New York in 1945. (courtesy National Museum of American History at the Smithsonian Institute)

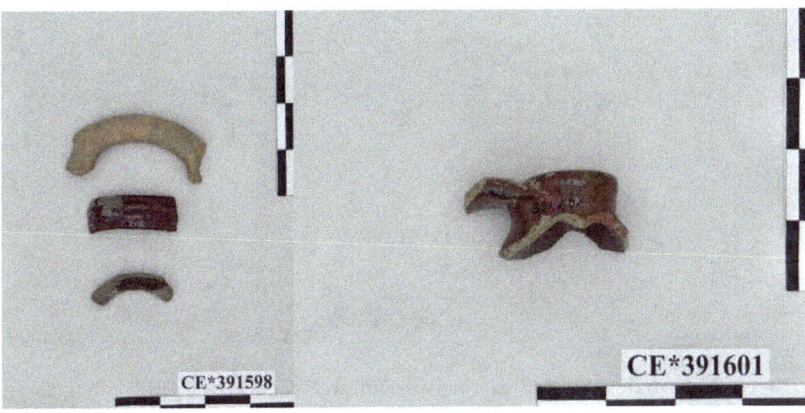

Figure 6.21 Red earthenware handles and a rim sherd with a partially attached handle from a jug recovered by Lura Woodside Watkins at the site of the Cornell Pottery in De Ruyter, New York in 1945. (courtesy National Museum of American History at the Smithsonian Institute)

A Celebrated Industry

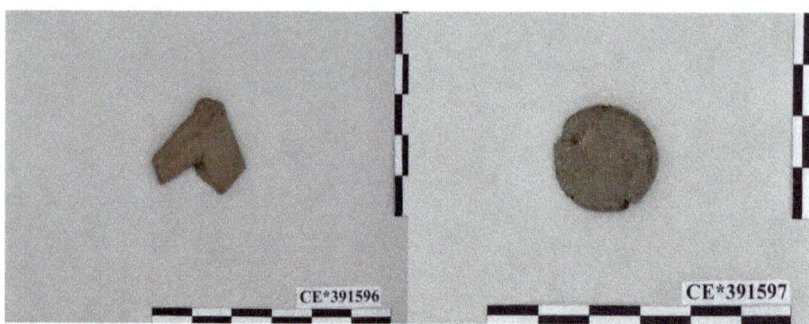

Figure 6.22 Red earthenware kiln furniture recovered by Lura Woodside Watkins at the site of the Cornell Pottery in De Ruyter, New York in 1945. (courtesy National Museum of American History at the Smithsonian Institute)

Figure 6.23 Remains of a red earthenware inkwell recovered by Lura Woodside Watkins at the site of the Cornell Pottery in De Ruyter, New York in 1945. (courtesy National Museum of American History at the Smithsonian Institute)

> Chapter 7

The Bradford Pottery in West Barnstable, Mass. on Cape Cod

Lura Woodside Watkins noted a pottery established by Noah Bradford (1761-1832) in West Barnstable, Massachusetts about 1819 in *Early New England Potters and Their Wares*, but the facts at the time seem to have been limited to a narrow history known about this business. Although, it must be noted that prior to Noah's arrival on Cape Cod that he was an accomplished potter working with his family in Kingston, Massachusetts.

It was published that the Noah Bradford who operated this company may have been Bradford's son, Noah Bradford Junior (1828-1905) who was also a potter; however, that information seems questionable seeing that it has been published in multiple sources that the elder Noah Bradford was in fact the man operating a pottery in West Barnstable. For instance, author Donald G. Trayser (1902-1955) wrote *Barnstable: Three Centuries of a Cape Cod Town,* published in 1939, stating, "*In West Barnstable a pottery was successfully carried on through the 1820s. Before that time the Cape had been supplied (partially) from Plymouth potteries (likely the Bradford Pottery in Kingston), but breakage in transportation was excessive. Noah Bradford, born in Kingston in 1761, learned and practiced his trade there. In 1819, he bought off Prince Nye (b. 1781), a piece of land with a potter's shop thereon. He may have leased the land previously and built the shop, or there may have been a potter before him. For at least ten years he made pottery here until his health failed. In the Patriot, July 18, 1832, Daniel Parker Junior*

A Celebrated Industry

(1771-1847), informed the public that he had taken the stand of the late Noah Bradford and he would supply Cape towns with earthenware made from the hands of the potter who for years had superintended the establishment."

The business then descended through the Parker family to Benjamin Parker before it was sold. Although, the most prominent years of production took place under Noah Bradford's ownership. Records indicate that the Parkers saw very little financial success, and they may have used the pottery as a means to supplement their yearly income.

While wares from the Bradford-Parker Pottery were apparently skilled, the business has been a subject of misinterpretation by some early collectors. For example, a small group of objects were displayed from the collection of Mr. and Mrs. William Whitman Junior, but also published in an antique exhibition catalog in Boston in 1925, attributing those objects to Barnstable. Author John Spargo (1876-1966) must have visited this exhibit since he then published the so-called Barnstable products in 1926 in *Early American Pottery and China.* Without more information, it is believed that most of these objects probably originated with the potteries that operated in Bristol County, Massachusetts. Instead, these objects were likely found in Barnstable, considering that the potters along the Taunton River are known to have exported their wares throughout the region and Rhode Island. However, there was a green glazed flowerpot included in the exhibit of particular interest.

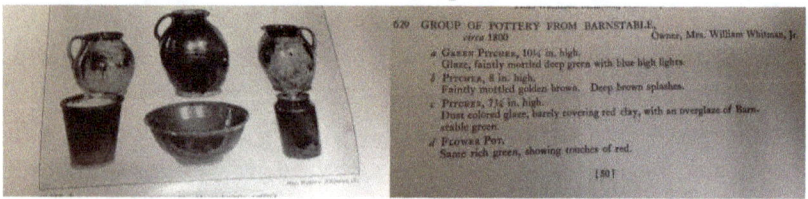

Figure 7.1 Wares attributed to West Barnstable on Cape Cod by author John Spargo in 1926 and at an antiques exhibit in Boston in 1925, although without more evidence, most of these objects are actually from Bristol County, Mass.

Although, it was published by Lura Woodside Watkins in *Early New England Potters and Their Wares* that a green glaze, often found on flowerpots, previously attributed to the Bradford-

Parker Pottery was unfounded and more likely produced by the potteries in Berkeley or Somerset. On the other hand, the site of this pottery was visited in the twentieth century by Sagamore, Massachusetts antiques dealer and former art director of the Heritage Museums and Gardens on Cape Cod, Brian Cullity, where the current property owners had begun construction for a swimming pool. Cullity was able to salvage a large number of artifacts from the pottery, which were likely found in land that was undisturbed prior to construction of the swimming pool, possibly within an 1820s context. This evidence includes all areas of pottery production, such as wasters, kiln bricks and kiln furniture. The artifacts also include the same green glazed flowerpot sherds that had been previously questioned, although a larger sample is probably needed to definitely say whether this type of production was made in West Barnstable, Bristol County or the documented green glazed flowerpots made by the Bradfords in Kingston (Chapter 3).

Interestingly, Henry Francis du Pont (1880-1969) acquired six green glazed flowerpot saucers and two flowerpots for Winterthur Museum in Delaware, which match this type of production. These objects were likely acquired when the green glazed wares from southeastern Massachusetts became popular with collectors in the 1920s and 1930s.

A similar and likely related flowerpot of interest with attached saucer and manufactured with a ruffled or crimped rim (Figure 8.17) is kept in the William T. Brandon Memorial Collection of American Redware and Ceramics at Historic Deerfield in Deerfield, Massachusetts. The pot retains an old note written on the base in pencil, which reads, *"Mrs. S.A. Parker / Barnstable / Cape Cod Pottery."* Characteristics found on this pot also match the archaeological evidence recovered by Cullity, along with some of the flowerpots from Kingston.

Other than the green glazed flowerpot sherds and saucers, the archaeological evidence confirms that the Bradford-Parker Pottery was a skilled business, much like their colleagues in Kingston. The evidence reveals an emphasis devoted to the production of colorful glazes, as well as black glazes, and some of the artifacts even demonstrate the use of wavy and straight-line

A Celebrated Industry

comb decoration, applied on the exterior of pots. Much like the business in Kingston, the wares made in West Barnstable likely embraced many of the expected forms from coastal Massachusetts pottery production of the period.

Preserved in the ceramic storage department at Old Sturbridge Village in Sturbridge, Massachusetts is a wonderful nineteenth century black glazed ovoid red earthenware jar with two unusual applied handles. Without knowing its history, this jar would likely be attributed to a number of locations in New England, and it may be connected to a style of squat ovoid jug infrequently found in collections. But the history that this object retains explains why this jar is of particular interest today.

The records at Old Sturbridge Village indicate that this jar descended in the family of Samuel Wing (1774-1854), a cabinetmaker in Sandwich, Massachusetts. Wing was born in Sandwich on October 12, 1774, and was of Quaker faith. Wing's shop was described in the book *Harbor and Home: Furniture of Southeastern Massachusetts, 1710-1850,* as a space measuring twenty by twelve and one-half feet, which may very well have been the standard for rural cabinetmakers of the period.

Wing's production included chairs, beds, yarn wheels, tables, and knife boxes. Some of the chairs were even painted green, a color of paint also used on furniture manufactured in southeastern Massachusetts and Rhode Island. This may have been a popular color for the region, seeing it was also a prolific glaze applied on some of the area's (and New England's) most dramatic pieces of red earthenware.

Upon Samuel's death in 1854, many of his possessions remained with family members, and descended through the Wings until Asa S. Wing, Samuel's great grandson donated most of the artisan's tools,

Figure 7.2 Two jars possibly made at the Bradford-Parker Pottery in West Barnstable, Mass. One retains a history of ownership with Sandwich, Mass. cabinetmake Samuel Wing. See Figure 7.7b. (courtesy Old Sturbridge Village)

A Celebrated Industry

patterns, equipment, among other possessions to Old Sturbridge Village in 1965. Mixed in with all of these objects was the black glazed red earthenware jar that I just described.

Even though this exact form has not been recovered at the site of the Bradford-Parker Pottery in West Barnstable, it should not be ruled out, either since the distance from the pottery to Wing's shop would have only been a matter of a few miles. The archaeological evidence also likely does not represent all production.

Even so, it should be noted that a few other matching jars have also been discovered in the Barnstable and Sandwich area over the years, including a second example owned by Old Sturbridge Village. Additionally, these objects are also related to a few other jar forms in existence, manufactured with distinct matching handles.

Another object of particular interest is a large pitcher also from the William T. Brandon Memorial Collection of American Redware and Ceramics at Historic Deerfield. This is one of a small group of these pitchers known to exist today, although, it retains an old tag, reading, *"Attributed to Barnstable Pottery. Coll'd 1918, West Barnstable, Mass."* But the pitcher is more likely from Bristol County.

Figure 7.3 Late eighteenth or early nineteenth century red earthenware pitcher most likely made in Bristol County, Mass., although an old tag identifies it as being made at the "Barnstable Pottery." (courtesy Historic Deerfield)

If nothing else, it is empowering to know that the Bradfords are direct descendants of William Bradford, an English separatist who migrated to the Plymouth Colony on the Mayflower in 1620. That is far from the end of their story.

The Bradfords were a skilled family of potters, who began practicing their craft before the American Revolution, and they continued to provide for the Plymouth area and Cape Cod well into the nineteenth century. For some reason, though the history of much of this production has been misplaced in time, despite the family business having actively produced local household utilitarian pottery for more than 100 years in separate locations in Massachusetts. I also suspect that some of this production may have been shipped elsewhere throughout Boston's South Shore and southeastern Massachusetts, as well as locations on Cape Cod.

Figure 7.4 Pan attributed to the Bradford Pottery on Cape Cod. (courtesy Heritage Museums and Gardens)

In the time that Lura Woodside Watkins examined the Bradford-Parker Pottery in *Early New England Potters and Their Ware*, she states, *"It must be remembered that a green color was not the monopoly of any potter; it was used in Portland, Maine, in Essex County, Massachusetts, and other places."* The most famous of these New England green glazes today is certainly the remarkable wares made along the Taunton River in Bristol County in the late eighteenth and nineteenth century.

Nevertheless, a very similar green glaze may have also been produced in West Barnstable, such a glaze that demonstrates further proof of the ability, accomplishments and experience found with Noah Bradford and possibly the Parkers. The inspiration for such a glaze may have been a result of the wares made in Bristol County and elsewhere in the region, but that statement may never be proven. Although, what is known is that they were producing skillfully thrown pottery in West Barnstable in the 1800s. But Watkins also wrote that green glazes were produced in Kingston, so the use of this glaze color may have also been a natural transition from what Noah Bradford was already familiar with to how he produced wares on Cape Cod in the 1820s.

Figure 7.5 Nineteenth century red earthenware jar related to the jars illustrated in Figure 7.2 and possibly made in West Barnstable, Mass. Inset photo shows the handle found on the these jars.

Figure 7.6 This jar was made with the exact same handles as the jars illustrated in Figures 7.2 and 7.5. (courtesy Sam Herrup).

A Celebrated Industry

Figure 7.7a-7.7b (Top) Jar found in Sandwich, Mass. on Cape Cod that matches the form of the jars owned by Old Sturbridge Village in Figure 7.2. (Below) A comparison of this jar with one of the jars at Old Sturbridge Village that is shown to the right. (courtesy Kris Casucci)

A Celebrated Industry

Figure 7.8a-7.8b This jar was made with the exact same handles as the jars illustrated in Figures 7.2, 7.5, 7.6 and 7.7a.

Figure 7.8c Another view of the jar.

A Celebrated Industry

Figure 7.9a-7.9b This jar was made with the exact same handles as the jars illustrated in Figures 7.2, 7.5, 7.6 , 7.7a, 7.8a, 7.8b and 7.8c.

Figure 7.10 A comparison of the jar shown in Figure 7.9a-7.9b with the jar shown in Figure 7.7a-7.7b. (courtesy Kris Casucci)

> Chapter 8

The Archaeology of the Barnstable Pottery

Until the nineteenth century came about Cape Cod was pretty much entirely dependent on domestic red earthenware imports from various New England manufacturers, likely businesses in Bristol County and wares manufactured in Charlestown, Massachusetts before the American Revolution. For instance, John Parker (1725-1765), an important potter from Charlestown kept a potter's daybook from 1747-1761 now owned by the Baker Library at Harvard University. According to this account book, Mr. James Lewes from Barnstable purchased seven wholesale orders of red earthenware in 1750 and 1751, and Mr. John Smith from Harwich purchased some wholesale shipments of red earthenware in 1751, as well. This pottery was then likely sold to local residents living on Cape Cod.

Another example is published in the book *Unearthing New England's Past: The Ceramic Evidence*, where it is written, "*Until the first quarter of the eighteenth century, the Cape Cod village of Welfleet participated in a thriving offshore whaling industry. Although the livelihood of residents including fishing, oyster harvesting, and agriculture, the hunting of black fish, or whales, was a key element in the regional economy.*

Local tradition claimed that a tavern was located on Great Island in Welfleet Harbor, but written records may have proven that it may have been lost in a nineteenth century fire at the Barnstable County Courthouse; archaeological evidence

A Celebrated Industry

suggests, however that there was a tavern on the island, but it may have been associated with whaling, perhaps as a way station.

Excavations revealed the stone foundation of a large building, fifty by thirty feet, with a central brick chimney. Typical of late seventeenth century New England vernacular construction, the main portion of the structure consisted of two rooms on either side of the chimney. A lean-to was probably attached at the rear.

Ceramics were the most significant artifacts in terms of both quantity and variety. Vessels associated with both food and beverage consumption, food storage, preparation and cooking were represented. Local red earthenware, some with distinctive slip decoration, predominated the collection."

Among the slipware was a sherd adorned with a type of slip design that can likely be traced back to the Parker family pottery in Charlestown, circa 1714-1755. This is also a similar timeframe as the sherd recovered in Welfleet, which was described by archaeologists as being recovered from a mid-eighteenth century archaeological context. Interestingly, the distance between Wellfleet and Barnstable is roughly thirty-four miles, while Wellfleet is separated from Harwich by about twenty-two miles, so it is unclear if there is any relationship with the order cited in Parker's daybook or if this was just from another source of Charlestown pottery that made its way into the Wellfleet area.

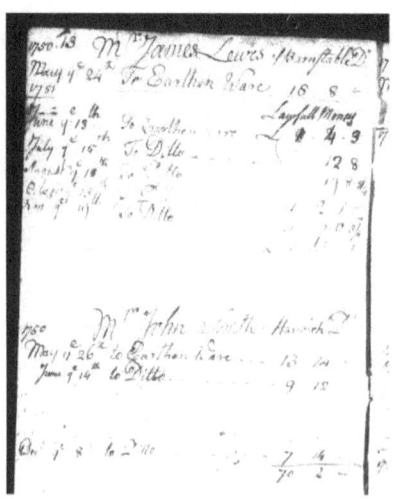

Figure 8.1 A page from John Parker's 1747-1761 potter's daybook indicating multiple orders of Charlestown pottery were shipped to Cape Cod in 1750 and 1751. (courtesy Baker Library at Harvard University)

A Celebrated Industry

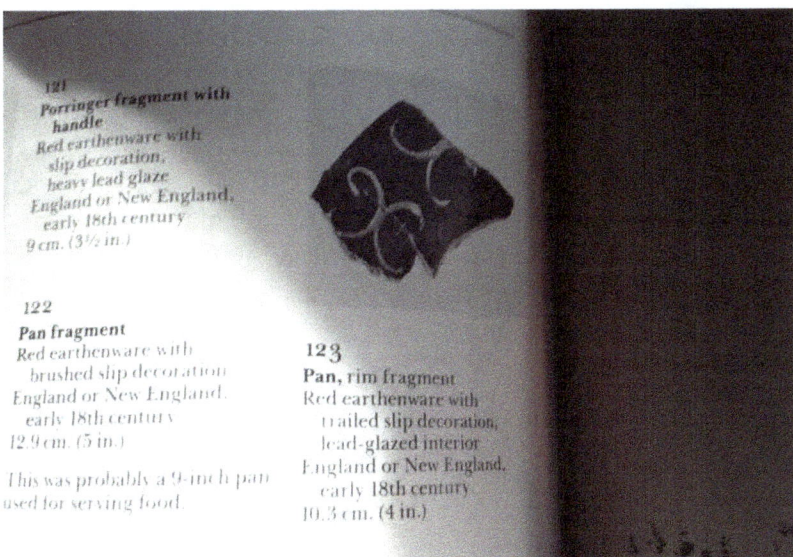

Figure 8.2 Charlestown, Mass. slip decorated red earthenware recovered in Welfleet, Mass. on Cape Cod. (Courtesy Unearthing New England's Past: The Ceramic Evidence)

Figure 8.3 Eighteenth century slip decorated red earthenware sherd recovered at the site of the Parker Pottery in Charlestown, Mass. This decoration matches the example found in Welfleet on Cape Cod. (courtesy City of Boston Archaeology Program)

183

A Celebrated Industry

Among the other eighteenth century contexts where domestic red earthenware has been recovered on Cape Cod is a collection of sherds found in Bourne. They were recovered when a home was demolished at 19 County Road, and apparently very close to the Apetucket Trading Post, a documented stagecoach stop and within walking distance of the Cape Cod Canal. The artifacts include a slip decorated red earthenware bowl, possibly of eighteenth-century origin, and very similar to wares made in Charlestown.

Figure 8.4 Eighteenth century slip decorated bowl recovered at a home in Bourne, Mass. on Cape Cod. (courtesy Vince Martonis)

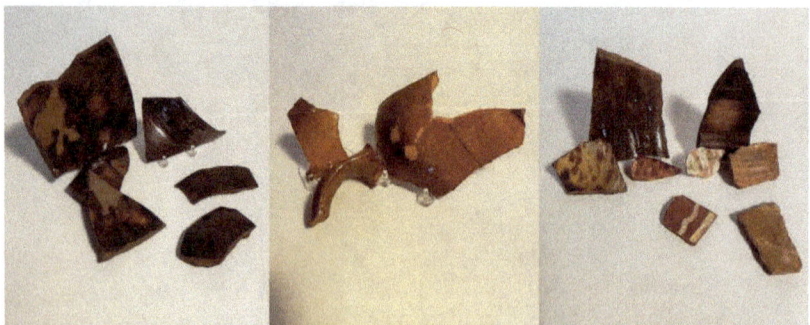

Figure 8.5 Other domestic red earthenware objects likely eighteenth century in origin recovered at a home in Bourne, Mass. on Cape Cod. (courtesy Vince Martonis)

A Celebrated Industry

There are also reports that the Bradfords in Kingston, Massachusetts were shipping red earthenware to Cape Cod, possibly in the eighteenth century, but documented in the nineteenth century. As written in the previous chapter, author Donald G. Trayser wrote *Barnstable: Three Centuries of a Cape Cod Town,* published in 1939, stating, *"In West Barnstable a pottery was successfully carried on through the 1820s. Before that time the Cape had been supplied (partially) from Plymouth potteries (likely the Bradford Pottery in Kingston), but breakage in transportation was excessive. Noah Bradford, born in Kingston in 1761, learned and practiced his trade there. In 1819, he bought off Prince Nye (b. 1781), a piece of land with a potter's shop thereon. He may have leased the land previously and built the shop, or there may have been a potter before him. For at least ten years he made pottery here until his health failed. In the Patriot, July 18, 1832, Daniel Parker Junior (1771-1847), informed the public that he had taken the stand of the late Noah Bradford and he would supply Cape towns with earthenware made from the hands of the potter who for years had superintended the establishment."*

The business then descended through the Parker family to Benjamin Parker before it was sold. This was likely Cape Cod's first red earthenware business, and because of Brian Cullity, a former art director at the Heritage Museums and Gardens on Cape Cod, a number of sherds and kiln evidence were saved from the site of the West Barnstable Pottery when construction for a swimming pool began in the twentieth century. The artifacts include a very similar green glaze when compared to the green glazes of Bristol County, and this type of green glaze was recovered at the site of the Bradford Pottery in Kingston, as well.

However, the green glaze recovered in West Barnstable is related to a type of flowerpot and flowerpot saucer production that has been debated through the years, whether it was made in Kingston, West Barnstable, Bristol County or all of the locations. Some of the rims on these objects are also ruffled, including some unrelated artifacts recovered in Somerset, Bristol County, Massachusetts (Figure 8.20) by Lura Woodside Watkins. This evidence is noteworthy, but a larger sample is likely needed to actually prove where this production took place. These types of floral wares are also found in private collections and museums around the country today, including Historic Deerfield in Deerfield, Massachusetts, the Little Compton, Rhode Island Historical Society, and Wintertur in Delaware. There were plenty of other glaze colors recovered, as well.

Archaeological evidence also reveals that a number of heavily thrown pots only glazed on the interior were produced in West Barnstable. But they were also manufacturing wares with decorative incised lines on the exterior, as well as using incised numbers, possibly to match a lidded jar or pot to the correct lid with the same number after it had been fired in the kiln. A similar type of numbering system was also used on some wares manufactured in Bristol County about the same period (Figure 8.24).

Figure 8.6a-8.6b There was also a brickyard in West Barnstable in the late 1800s supplying a lot of Cape Cod with red bricks. (courtesy Whelden Memorial Library)

A Celebrated Industry

Figure 8.7a-8.7b 1866 Main Route 6A Street, West Barnstable, Mass. Two of the bricks in the home's fireplace are marked "W BARNSTABLE BRICK CO." A marked brick can also be found on the exterior of the Marston's Mills Post Office in Barnstable, Mass.

Figure 8.8 (Left) Ruins of the West Barnstable Brick Co., and (Right) bricks can be found all around this area.

A Celebrated Industry

Figure 8.9 Various red earthenware artifacts recovered at the site of the Bradford-Parker Pottery in West Barnstable on Cape by Brian Cullity – much of the production represented here is utilitarian pots and pans only glazed on the interior.

Figure 8.10 Kiln furniture recovered by Brian Cullity at the site of the Bradford-Parker Pottery in West Barnstable on Cape Cod.

A Celebrated Industry

Figure 8.11a Among the artifacts recovered at the West Barnstable Pottery was archaeological evidence showing this type of green glazed flowerpot saucer was recovered there, probably within an 1820s context. This type of saucer went along with a green glazed flowerpot. This type of production is typically attributed to Bristol County today, although a larger sample is likely needed for an accurate answer to say where these type of objects were made. This type of flowerpot and saucer was also made in Kingston, Mass.

Figure 8.11b Among the artifacts recovered at the West Barnstable Pottery was archaeological evidence showing this type of green glazed flowerpot saucer was recovered there, probably within an 1820s context. This type of saucer went along with a green glazed flowerpot. This type of production is typically attributed to Bristol County today, although a larger sample is likely needed for an accurate answer to say where these type of objects were made. This type of flowerpot and saucer was also made in Kingston, Mass.

A Celebrated Industry

Figure 8.11c Among the artifacts recovered at the West Barnstable Pottery was archaeological evidence showing this type of green glazed flowerpot saucer was recovered there, probably within an 1820s context. This type of saucer went along with a green glazed flowerpot. This type of production is typically attributed to Bristol County today, although a larger sample is likely needed for an accurate answer to say where these type of objects were made. This type of flowerpot and saucer was also made in Kingston, Mass.

Figure 8.12 Sherds from other green glazed forms were also recovered at the site of the West Barnstable Pottery.

A Celebrated Industry

Figure 8.13 This is some of the collection of these type of green glazed flowerpot saucers collected by Henry Francis Dupont in the twentieth century. These type of flowerpot saucers are also illustrated in Figures 3.3-3.4. (courtesy Winterthur)

Figure 8.14 More examples of these type of green glazed flowerpot saucers, which were previously owned by Hilary & Paulette Nolan and the third by Brian Cullity. These type of flowerpot saucers are also illustrated in Figures 3.3-3.4.

Figure 8.15 Another related green glazed red earthenware flowerpot and saucer. (courtesy Skinner)

A Celebrated Industry

Figure 8.16 Another example of this type of green glazed flowerpot saucer. These type of flowerpot saucers are also illustrated in Figures 3.3-3.4. (courtesy Little Compton, Rhode Island Historical Society)

Figure 8.17 Nineteenth century green glazed red earthenware flowerpot with attached saucer identified on the base as being made in Barnstable at the Cape Cod Pottery. (courtesy Historic Deerfield)

A Celebrated Industry

Figure 8.18-8.19 Another example of this type of green glazed flowerpot saucer. An example very similar to this one is owned by Winterthur. These type of flowerpot saucers are also illustrated in Figures 3.3-3.4. The glaze on this piece is also similar to the sherd illustrated in Figures 8.20a-8.20b. (courtesy Bill Taylor)

A Celebrated Industry

Figure 8.20a-8.20b Circa 1790-1830 green and plum glazed red earthenware sherd with a ruffled rim recovered by Lura Woodside Watkins in Somerset, Bristol County, Mass. (courtesy National Museum of American History at the Smithsonian Institute)

A Celebrated Industry

Figure 8.21 Sherds with incised exterior designs were also recovered at the site of the Bradford-Parker Pottery in West Barnstable on Cape Cod.

Figure 8.22 Sherds with incised numbers were also recovered at the site of the Bradford-Parker Pottery in West Barnstable on Cape Cod.

A Celebrated Industry

Figure 8.23 This sherd with incised number recovered at the site of the Bradford-Parker Pottery in West Barnstable on Cape Cod may be related to this jar thought to have been made there, as well, also illustrated in Figures 7.8a, 7.8b and and 7.8c.

Figure 8.24 The potters in Bristol County, Mass. also used incised number on the exterior of pots, such as this example. The numbers were often used to match the correct lid that would have had the same incised number. (courtesy Ron & Penny Dionne Collection and Antiques Associates at West Townsend)

A Celebrated Industry

Figure 8.25 Potters elsewhere in America also inscribed numbers on the exterior of objects in a similar manner, such as this pot that may have been made in western New York possibly by Carl Mehwaldt (1809-1887) in Bergholz, Niagara County, New York. The Safford family was also known for this in Monmouth, Maine.

A Celebrated Industry

Figure 8.26 Nineteenth century red earthenware jar inscribed with the number "7" on the side and the lid appears to be inscribed with the number "15" on the top. It is unknown to the author if this piece is related to the Bradfords or another American manufacturer. The jar was found year ago in central Massachusetts.

A Celebrated Industry

Figure 8.27 Nineteenth century New England red earthenware handled pot inscribed with the number "24" on one side.

A Celebrated Industry

Figure 8.28 Nineteenth century green glazed red earthenware flowerpot and saucer that is similar in production to some of the other objects illustrated in this chapter. (courtesy Historic Deerfield)

Figure 8.29 Two nineteenth century green glazed red earthenware flowerpots owned by Historic New England that were acquired by the museum from Margaret H. Jewell (1866-1970). Each retains a lengthy history of ownership in New England. (courtesy Historic New England)

A Celebrated Industry

Nye Family Homestead Archaeology in Sandwich, Mass.

Figure 8.30 An aerial photo of the Nye family homestead in Sandwich, Mass. (courtesy Oakwood Photography by James R. Walczak)

Figure 8.31 Collection of red earthenware sherds and other nineteenth century ceramic artifacts collected at the Nye House in Sandwich, Mass. Some of the red earthenware may have been made in nearby West Barnstable, Mass. The museum also owns a slipware dish from Bristol County, Mass. (courtesy Nye Museum)

A Celebrated Industry

Figure 8.32 A red earthenware milk pan and a red earthenware potsherd found on the east side of the Nye property where the original kitchen and buttery were located. (courtesy Nye Museum)

Figure 8.33 Eighteenth or early nineteenth century slip decorated red earthenware dish attributed to Bristol County, Mass. (courtesy Nye Museum)

> Chapter 9

The Historical Significance of the Potteries in Southeastern Massachusetts, Bristol County and Cape Cod

There's really no explanation needed after seeing the objects illustrated throughout this book to understand why this region's production from the eighteenth and nineteenth century is considered to be at the forefront of domestic red earthenware production, especially during the late eighteenth and early nineteenth century period, circa 1780-1830. This region's production has it all: refinement, skill, form, glaze and the aesthetics, essentially transforming much of this everyday utilitarian production into works of art, which can easily be displayed at any art museum in America.

I thought an appropriate way to conclude this book was to share a narrative that was written by former art director of the Heritage Museums and Gardens on Cape Cod and Sagamore, Massachusetts antiques dealer Brian Cullity. He wrote this for when Falmouth, Massachusetts antiques dealers, Hilary and Paulette Nolan's lifelong red earthenware collection sold at Northeast Auctions in Manchester, New Hampshire in the summer of 2004.

"*Collecting Americana has been a passion in this country for well over 100 years, yet it is only within the past two of three decades, that the beauty, form and rarity of New England red* earthenware has registered with most contemporary collectors and dealers. Hilary and Paulette Nolan were fortunate to have been inspired thirty years ago by the singular elegance and splendor of these utilitarian objects and the ensuing years have resulted in a grouping of eye dazzling beauty. Their attention on the truly magnificent symmetry, form, and above all the colors achieved by the eighteenth and nineteenth century New England potters is a testament to their collection and focus in assemblage of this significant collection.

As with any collecting journey, insights and revelations would build an awareness and deeper understanding of the artists, who created these pieces and parts of the puzzle would fall into place as time progressed. While the majority of the Nolan Collection is focused on Bristol County, some outstanding pieces of other regional New England centers are also to be found in the collection. Rare forms with a rainbow of colors came from a diversity of sources, from old time dealers such as I.M. Wiese, to pieces found at local flea markets or even the town landfill.

Charlotte Cook of Little Compton, Rhode Island was an early source and fountain of knowledge. Mrs. Clark of New Bedford, while no longer living in the 1970s certainly helped with establishing the importance and desirability of these ceramic objects. Most likely, the Nolans have concluded, it was her marketing of redware through her shop in New Bedford in the first half of the twentieth century that cemented the name "New Bedford Pottery" into the lexicon of the antiques world. Her son, who Hilary and Paulette met in Rhode Island confirmed that the bright orange crayon prices found on the bottom of some pieces were placed there by Mrs. Clark. Surprisingly these were not cheap prices even then.

The information that accompanies each object and written by the Nolans contains valuable information on provenance and their personal insights on various pieces. What they have not included are the resounding accolades of friends and associates, scientists, fishermen and the casual visitor who have all responded in a similar manner to this outstanding collection. One need not to be an antiquarian to appreciate the timeless beauty of these art objects. They speak to anyone who takes the time to

A Celebrated Industry

stand back and enjoy the fruits of our gifted ancestor's craftsmanship and artistry."

Figure 9.1 Bristol County red earthenware displayed as part of Brian Cullity's exhibit at the Heritage Museums and Garden on Cape Cod, titled, Slipped and Glazed: Regional American Redware.

A Celebrated Industry

Figure 9.2-9.3 Some pieces formerly owned by Hilary and Paulette Nolan. The base of each piece retains a jelly label that Paulette wrote notes on about the object.

A Celebrated Industry

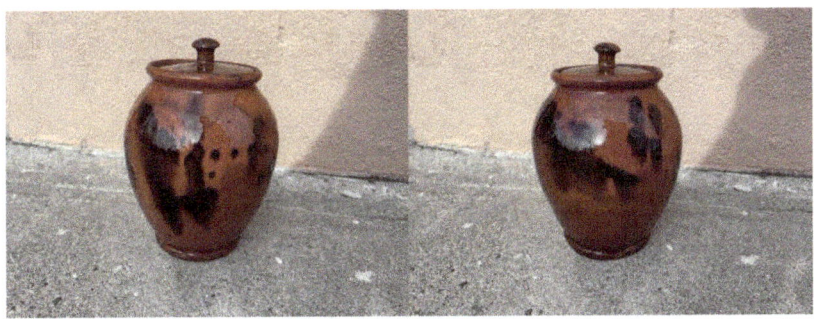

Figure 9.4 Late eighteenth or early nineteenth century red earthenware jar formerly owned by Hilary and Paulette Nolan. The lid is not original and probably from Maine. (courtesy Ross Levett)

A Celebrated Industry

Figure 9.5 While Martha's Vineyard and Nantucket are not thought to have been places where early red earthenware production took place, an important brick making factory did exist on Martha's Vineyard. The Chilmark Brickyard was established on the island's north shore in 1642 and passed through multiple owners until it was decommissioned in the late 1800s. Interestingly, utilitarian red earthenware made in Bristol County, Mass., Charlestown, Mass. and Philadelphia have all been recovered from various archaeological contexts on the island. (courtesy Martha's Vineyard Museum)

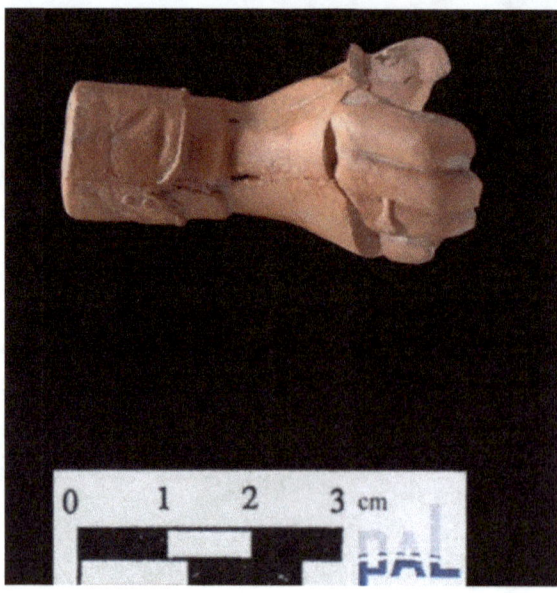

Figure 9.6 Red earthenware pipe in the shape of a hand possibly made at the Chilmark Brickyard. Recovered by archaeologists during the Gay Head Archaeological Project on Martha's Vineyard. (courtesy PAL Archaeology)

> Illustrations

Note: Unless otherwise indicated, all of the wares manufactured in southeastern Massachusetts, Bristol County and Cape Cod are unglazed or decorated with a lead glaze, multiple glaze colors and various types of slip decoration. The majority of these pieces are not signed by the potter, although the few marked pieces are noted. It is also important to understand that while many of these objects were manufactured in the early nineteenth century, I describe most as being produced in the late eighteenth or early nineteenth century, circa 1780-1830.

A Celebrated Industry

> Partially Glazed Household Wares

1) Eighteenth or nineteenth century red earthenware pots glazed only on the interior possibly from southeastern Massachusetts, Bristol County or Cape Cod. (courtesy Little Compton, Rhode Island Historical Society)

> Animal Wares

2) Red earthenware bird bottle possibly made in southeastern Massachusetts, Bristol County or Cape Cod. (courtesy Little Compton, Rhode Island Historical Society

A Celebrated Industry

> Flowerpots

3) Nineteenth century hanging green glazed red earthenware flowerpot with attached saucer possibly made in southeastern Massachusetts, Bristol County or Cape Cod, otherwise another American manufacturer. (courtesy Winterthur)

A Celebrated Industry

> Marriage Jars & Other Significant Pieces

4) Nineteenth century slip decorated red earthenware marriage jars made at the Purinton Pottery in Somerset, Bristol County, Massachusetts in 1809 for George and Debby Purinton. (courtesy Metropolitan Museum of Art)

A Celebrated Industry

5-6) Additional views of the marriage jars. (courtesy Metropolitan Museum of Art)

A Celebrated Industry

7-8) Additional views of the marriage jars. (courtesy Metropolitan Museum of Art)

A Celebrated Industry

9) Additional views of the marriage jars. (courtesy Metropolitan Museum of Art)

A Celebrated Industry

10) Additional views of the marriage jars. (courtesy Metropolitan Museum of Art)

A Celebrated Industry

11) My nephew Jason pictured with the marriage jars. (courtesy Metropolitan Museum of Art)

12) Nineteenth century slip decorated marriage or presentation jar made in Bristol County, Mass. The jar is dated "1812" under one handle with the initials "A.P." under the other. (courtesy Hilary & Paulette Nolan, as well as Slipped and Glazed: Regional American Redware)

A Celebrated Industry

13a-13b) Nineteenth century red earthenware presentation jar, dated "1829" and inscribed with initials in slip "APB" or "ASB" with quite a unique lid. This jar was featured on the cover of The Magazine Antiques October 1931 issue.

A Celebrated Industry

> Glazed Household Wares

14) Late eighteenth or early nineteenth century green glazed red earthenware jar attributed to Bristol County, Mass. (courtesy Northeast Auctions)

15) Late eighteenth or early nineteenth century red earthenware jar attributed to Bristol County, Mass. (courtesy Northeast Auctions)

A Celebrated Industry

16) Late eighteenth or early nineteenth century red earthenware jar attributed to Bristol County, Mass. (courtesy Northeast Auctions)

17) Late eighteenth or early nineteenth century red earthenware jar attributed to Bristol County, Mass. (courtesy Northeast Auctions)

A Celebrated Industry

18) Late eighteenth or early nineteenth century red earthenware jar most likely made in Bristol County, Mass. (courtesy Northeast Auctions)

A Celebrated Industry

19) Late eighteenth or early nineteenth century red earthenware jar attributed to Bristol County, Mass. (courtesy Northeast Auctions)

20) Late eighteenth or early nineteenth century green glaze red earthenware jar attributed to Bristol County, Mass. (courtesy Northeast Auctions)

A Celebrated Industry

21) Late eighteenth or early nineteenth century red earthenware jar attributed to Bristol County, Mass. (courtesy Ron & Penny Dionne Collection and Antiques Associates at West Townsend)

A Celebrated Industry

22) Late eighteenth or early nineteenth century red earthenware jar attributed to Bristol County, Mass. (courtesy Ron & Penny Dionne Collection and Antiques Associates at West Townsend)

23) Late eighteenth or early nineteenth century red earthenware jar attributed to Bristol County, Mass. (courtesy Ron & Penny Dionne Collection and Antiques Associates at West Townsend)

A Celebrated Industry

24) Late eighteenth or early nineteenth century red earthenware jar attributed to Bristol County, Mass. (courtesy Ron & Penny Dionne Collection and Antiques Associates at West Townsend)

A Celebrated Industry

25) Late eighteenth or early nineteenth century red earthenware jar attributed to Bristol County, Mass. (courtesy Ron & Penny Dionne Collection and Antiques Associates at West Townsend)

26) Late eighteenth or early nineteenth century red earthenware jar attributed to Bristol County, Mass. (courtesy Ron & Penny Dionne Collection and Antiques Associates at West Townsend)

A Celebrated Industry

27) Late eighteenth or early nineteenth century green glazed red earthenware jar attributed to Bristol County, Mass. (courtesy Ron & Penny Dionne Collection and Antiques Associates at West Townsend)

A Celebrated Industry

28) Late eighteenth or early nineteenth century red earthenware jar attributed to Bristol County, Mass. (courtesy Ron & Penny Dionne Collection and Antiques Associates at West Townsend)

A Celebrated Industry

29) Late eighteenth or early nineteenth century red earthenware jar attributed to Bristol County, Mass. that was found in an attic on Cape Cod by Hilary Nolan.

A Celebrated Industry

30) **Late eighteenth or early nineteenth century red earthenware jar attributed to Bristol County, Mass.**

A Celebrated Industry

31) Late eighteenth or early nineteenth century red earthenware jar attributed to Bristol County, Mass.

A Celebrated Industry

32) Late eighteenth or early nineteenth century red earthenware jar attributed to Bristol County, Mass. The base of the lid and jar are inscribed with matching Roman numerals, either "IX" or "XI."

A Celebrated Industry

33) Late eighteenth or early nineteenth century red earthenware jar attributed to Bristol County, Mass.

239

A Celebrated Industry

34) Late eighteenth or early nineteenth century red earthenware jar attributed to Bristol County, Mass. (courtesy Brian Trevorrow)

35) Late eighteenth or early nineteenth century red earthenware jar attributed to Bristol County, Mass. (courtesy Little Compton, Rhode Island Historical Society)

A Celebrated Industry

36) (Middle) Late eighteenth or early nineteenth century red earthenware jar attributed to Bristol County, Mass. (courtesy Roger Pheulpin)

37) Late eighteenth or early nineteenth century red earthenware jars attributed to Bristol County, Mass. (courtesy Lewis Scranton)

A Celebrated Industry

38) Late eighteenth or early nineteenth century red earthenware jar attributed to Bristol County, Mass. (courtesy Winterthur)

A Celebrated Industry

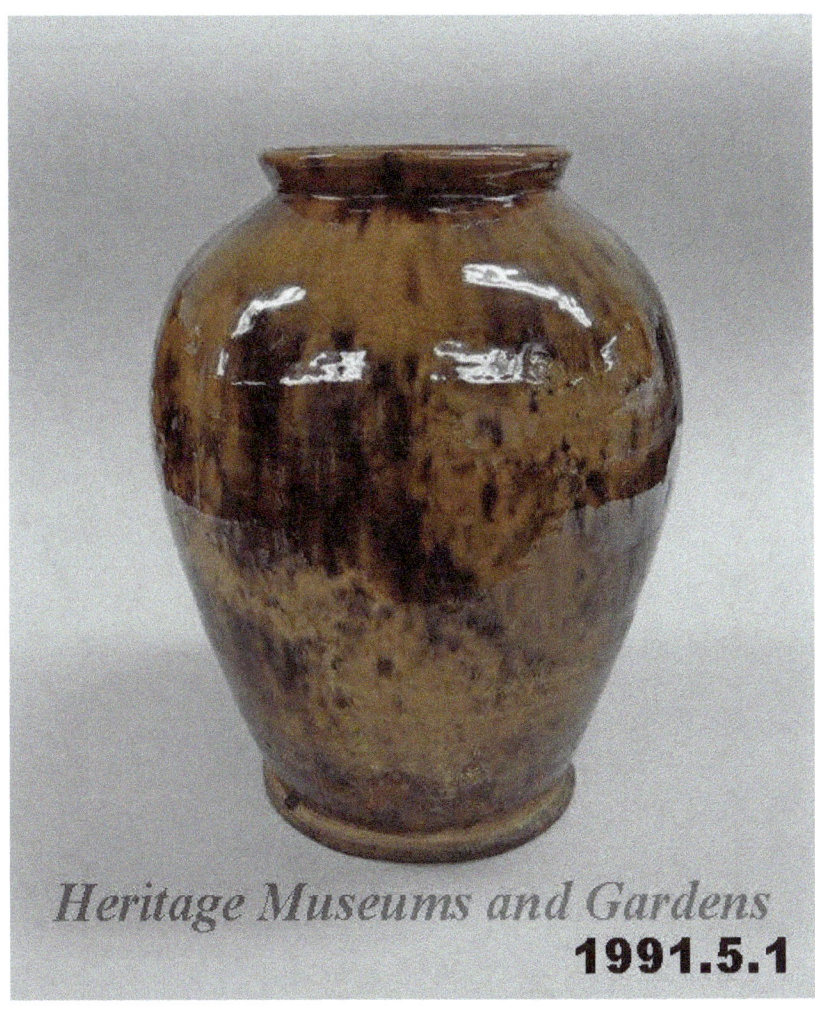

39) Late eighteenth or early nineteenth century red earthenware jar attributed to Bristol County, Mass. (courtesy Heritage Museums and Gardens)

40) Late eighteenth or early nineteenth century green glazed red earthenware jar attributed to Bristol County, Mass. (courtesy Heritage Museums and Gardens)

A Celebrated Industry

41) Late eighteenth or early nineteenth century red earthenware jar attributed to Bristol County, Mass. (courtesy Heritage Museums and Gardens)

A Celebrated Industry

42) (Right) Late eighteenth or early nineteenth century green glazed red earthenware jar attributed to Bristol County, Mass. (courtesy Christies)

43) (Left and Middle) Late eighteenth or early nineteenth century red earthenware jars attributed to Bristol County, Mass. (courtesy Christies)

44) (Left and Middle) Late eighteenth or early nineteenth century red earthenware jar attributed to Bristol County, Mass. The jar shown to the left is adorned with a slip decorated flower. (courtesy Christies)

A Celebrated Industry

45) Late eighteenth or early nineteenth century red earthenware jar attributed to either southeastern Massachusetts or Bristol County, Mass. It may also have been produced by John Henry Benner in Abington, Mass. (courtesy Historic New England)

46) Late eighteenth or early nineteenth century red earthenware jar attributed to either southeastern Massachusetts or Bristol County, Mass. (courtesy Tim Gould)

A Celebrated Industry

47) Late eighteenth or early nineteenth century red earthenware jar attributed to Bristol County, Mass.

A Celebrated Industry

48) Late eighteenth or early nineteenth century red earthenware jar attributed to Bristol County, Mass. (courtesy Sam Herrup)

49) Late eighteenth or early nineteenth century green glazed red earthenware jar attributed to Bristol County, Mass. (courtesy Sam Herrup)

A Celebrated Industry

50) Late eighteenth or early nineteenth century red earthenware jar attributed to Bristol County, Mass. (courtesy Sam Herrup)

51) Late eighteenth or early nineteenth century red earthenware jar and jug attributed to Bristol County, Mass. (courtesy Sam Herrup)

A Celebrated Industry

52) Late eighteenth or early nineteenth century red earthenware pitcher attributed to Bristol County, Mass. – notice the bottom half, it's a jar that was converted into a pitcher.

A Celebrated Industry

53) Late eighteenth or early nineteenth century red earthenware jar attributed to Bristol County, Mass., where some of the glaze has turned a rare pinkish color. (courtesy Sam Herrup)

54) Late eighteenth or early nineteenth century green glazed red earthenware jar attributed to Bristol County, Mass. (courtesy Little Compton, Rhode Island Historical Society)

A Celebrated Industry

55) Late eighteenth or early nineteenth century red earthenware jar attributed to Bristol County, Mass. (courtesy Lewis Scranton

A Celebrated Industry

56) Late eighteenth or early nineteenth century red earthenware jar attributed to Bristol County, Mass. (courtesy Tim Gould)

A Celebrated Industry

57) Late eighteenth or early nineteenth century red earthenware jar attributed to Bristol County, Mass. (courtesy Little Compton, Rhode Island Historical Society)

58) Late eighteenth or early nineteenth century red earthenware jar attributed to Bristol County, Mass.

A Celebrated Industry

59) Late eighteenth or early nineteenth century red earthenware jar attributed to Bristol County, Mass.

60) Late eighteenth or early nineteenth century green glazed red earthenware jar attributed to Bristol County, Mass. (courtesy Crocker Farm)

A Celebrated Industry

61) Late eighteenth or early nineteenth century red earthenware jar attributed to Bristol County, Mass.

A Celebrated Industry

62) Late eighteenth or early nineteenth century red earthenware jar attributed to Bristol County, Mass.

A Celebrated Industry

63) Late eighteenth or early nineteenth century red earthenware jars attributed to Bristol County, Mass., both reportedly retaining a history of descending through the Nye family of Nantucket.

A Celebrated Industry

64) Late eighteenth or early nineteenth century red earthenware jar attributed to Bristol County, Mass. (courtesy Hilary & Paulette Nolan Collection)

65) Late eighteenth or early nineteenth century red earthenware jars attributed to Bristol County, Mass.; Lura Woodside Watkins Collection. (courtesy National Museum of American History at the Smithsonian Institute)

A Celebrated Industry

66) Late eighteenth or early nineteenth century red earthenware jar attributed to Bristol County, Mass. (courtesy Winterthur)

A Celebrated Industry

67) Late eighteenth or early nineteenth century green glazed red earthenware jar attributed to Bristol County, Mass. (courtesy Winterthur)

A Celebrated Industry

68) Late eighteenth or early nineteenth century green glazed red earthenware jar attributed to Bristol County, Mass., shown to the right in the bottom photo. (courtesy Winterthur)

A Celebrated Industry

69) Late eighteenth or early nineteenth century green glazed red earthenware jar attributed to Bristol County, Mass., shown to the left in the bottom picture. (courtesy Winterthur)

A Celebrated Industry

70-71) Late eighteenth or early nineteenth century green glazed red earthenware jars attributed to Bristol County, Mass. (courtesy Skinner)

A Celebrated Industry

72) Late eighteenth or early nineteenth century red earthenware jar attributed to Bristol County, Mass. (courtesy Old Sturbridge Village)

73) Late eighteenth or early nineteenth century red earthenware jar attributed to Bristol County, Mass. (courtesy Old Sturbridge Village)

A Celebrated Industry

74) Late eighteenth or early nineteenth century red earthenware jar attributed to Bristol County, Mass. (courtesy Old Sturbridge Village)

75) Late eighteenth or early nineteenth century red earthenware jar attributed to Bristol County, Mass. (courtesy Old Sturbridge Village)

A Celebrated Industry

76) Late eighteenth or early nineteenth century red earthenware jar attributed to Bristol County, Mass. (courtesy Sam Herrup, former Hilary and Paulette Nolan Collection)

77) Late eighteenth or early nineteenth century red earthenware jar attributed to Bristol County, Mass. (courtesy Old Sturbridge Village)

A Celebrated Industry

78) Late eighteenth or early nineteenth century red earthenware jar attributed to Bristol County, Mass. (courtesy Sam Herrup)

A Celebrated Industry

79) Late eighteenth or early nineteenth century green glazed red earthenware jar likely made in either southeastern Massachusetts or Bristol County, Mass., formerly owned by Charles D. Cook. (courtesy Northeast Auctions)

A Celebrated Industry

80) Late eighteenth or early nineteenth century green glazed red earthenware jar likely made in either southeastern Massachusetts or Bristol County, Mass.

A Celebrated Industry

81) Late eighteenth or early nineteenth century red earthenware jar likely made in either southeastern Massachusetts or Bristol County, Mass. (courtesy Northeast Auctions)

A Celebrated Industry

82) Late eighteenth or early nineteenth century red earthenware jar likely made in either southeastern Massachusetts or Bristol County, Mass. (courtesy Ron & Penny Dionne Collection and Antiques Associates at West Townsend)

A Celebrated Industry

83-84) Late eighteenth or early nineteenth century red earthenware jars likely made in either southeastern Massachusetts or Bristol County, Mass.

A Celebrated Industry

85) Late eighteenth or early nineteenth century red earthenware jar attributed to Bristol County, Mass. (courtesy Northeast Auctions)

86) Late eighteenth or early nineteenth century red earthenware jar attributed to Bristol County, Mass. (courtesy Lewis Scranton and Skinner)

87) Late eighteenth or early nineteenth century red earthenware jar attributed to Bristol County, Mass. (courtesy Ron & Penny Dionne Collection and Antiques Associates at West Townsend)

A Celebrated Industry

88) Late eighteenth or early nineteenth century red earthenware jar attributed to Bristol County, Mass. (courtesy Crocker Farm)

A Celebrated Industry

89-90) Late eighteenth or early nineteenth century red earthenware jars attributed to Bristol County, Mass. (courtesy Northeast Auctions and Crocker Farm)

91) Late eighteenth or early nineteenth century red earthenware jar attributed to Bristol County, Mass. (courtesy Ron & Penny Dionne Collection and Antiques Associates at West Townsend)

A Celebrated Industry

92) Late eighteenth or early nineteenth century green glazed red earthenware jar attributed to Bristol County, Mass. (courtesy Northeast Auctions)

93) Late eighteenth or early nineteenth century green glazed red earthenware jar attributed to Bristol County, Mass. (courtesy Sam Herrup)

A Celebrated Industry

94) Late eighteenth or early nineteenth century green glazed red earthenware jar likely made in Bristol County, Mass.

95) Late eighteenth or early nineteenth century green glazed red earthenware jar attributed to Bristol County, Mass.; Lura Woodside Watkins Collection. (courtesy National Museum of American History at the Smithsonian Institute)

A Celebrated Industry

96) Late eighteenth or early nineteenth century red earthenware jar likely made in Bristol County, Mass.

97) Late eighteenth or early nineteenth century red earthenware jars likely made in Bristol County, Mass. (courtesy Lewis Scranton)

A Celebrated Industry

98) Late eighteenth or early nineteenth century red earthenware jar likely made in Bristol County, Mass. (courtesy Historic New England)

A Celebrated Industry

99) Late eighteenth or early nineteenth century green glazed red earthenware jar likely made in Bristol County, Mass.

A Celebrated Industry

100) Late eighteenth or early nineteenth century red earthenware jar likely made in Bristol County, Mass. (courtesy Old Sturbridge Village)

101) Late eighteenth or early nineteenth century red earthenware jar likely made in Bristol County, Mass. (courtesy Old Sturbridge Village)

A Celebrated Industry

102) Red earthenware jar probably eighteenth century in origin and probably manufactured in either Essex County, southeastern Massachusetts or Bristol County)

A Celebrated Industry

103) Late eighteenth or early nineteenth century red earthenware jug attributed to Bristol County, Mass. (courtesy Northeast Auctions)

104) Late eighteenth or early nineteenth century red earthenware jug attributed to Bristol County, Mass. (courtesy Jeff & Holly Noordsy)

105) Late eighteenth or early nineteenth century red earthenware jug attributed to Bristol County, Mass. (courtesy Northeast Auctions)

A Celebrated Industry

106) Late eighteenth or early nineteenth century red earthenware jug attributed to Bristol County, Mass. (courtesy Northeast Auctions)

A Celebrated Industry

107) Late eighteenth or early nineteenth century green glazed red earthenware jug attributed to Bristol County, Mass. (courtesy Northeast Auctions)

Figure 108) Late eighteenth or early nineteenth century green glazed red earthenware jug attributed to Bristol County, Mass. (courtesy Little Compton, Rhode Island Historical Society)

A Celebrated Industry

109) Late eighteenth or early nineteenth century red earthenware jug probably made in Bristol County, Mass. (courtesy Northeast Auctions)

110) Late eighteenth or early nineteenth century green glazed red earthenware jug attributed to Bristol County, Mass. (courtesy Ron & Penny Dionne Collection and Antiques Associates at West Townsend)

111) Late eighteenth or early nineteenth century green glazed red earthenware jug attributed to Bristol County, Mass. (courtesy Ron & Penny Dionne Collection and Antiques Associates at West Townsend)

A Celebrated Industry

112) Late eighteenth or early nineteenth century green glazed red earthenware jug attributed to Bristol County, Mass. (courtesy Ron & Penny Dionne Collection and Antiques Associates at West Townsend)

113) Late eighteenth or early nineteenth century red earthenware jug attributed to Bristol County, Mass. (courtesy Ron & Penny Dionne Collection and Antiques Associates at West Townsend)

A Celebrated Industry

114) Late eighteenth or early nineteenth century red earthenware jug attributed to Bristol County, Mass. (courtesy Ron & Penny Dionne Collection and Antiques Associates at West Townsend)

A Celebrated Industry

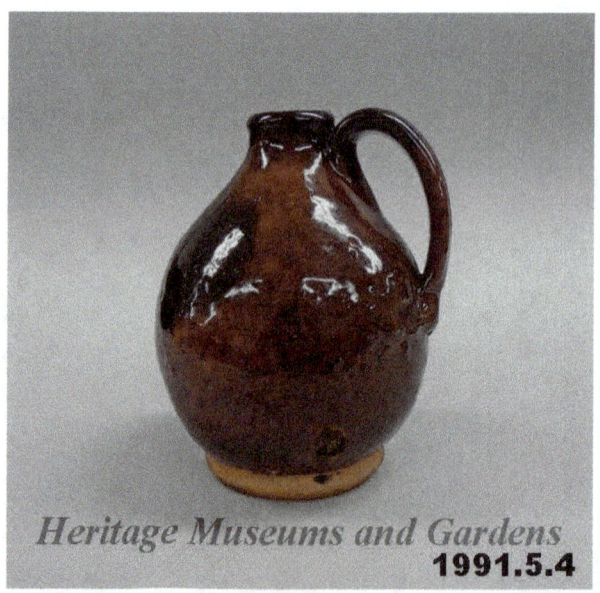

115) Late eighteenth or early nineteenth century red earthenware jug attributed to Bristol County, Mass. (courtesy Heritage Museums and Gardens)

116) Late eighteenth or early nineteenth century red earthenware jug attributed to Bristol County, Mass.

A Celebrated Industry

117) Late eighteenth or early nineteenth century green glazed red earthenware jug attributed to Bristol County, Mass.

A Celebrated Industry

118) Late eighteenth or early nineteenth century red earthenware jug attributed to Bristol County, Mass. (courtesy Sam Herrup)

A Celebrated Industry

119) Late eighteenth or early nineteenth century red earthenware jug attributed to Bristol County, Mass. (courtesy AAAWT, Hilary & Paulette Nolan Collection)

120) Late eighteenth or early nineteenth century red earthenware jug attributed to Bristol County, Mass. This glaze combined with the slip decoration is extremely rare today.

A Celebrated Industry

121) Late eighteenth or early nineteenth century black glazed red earthenware jugs attributed to Bristol County, Mass.

A Celebrated Industry

122) Late eighteenth or early nineteenth century green glazed red earthenware jug attributed to Bristol County, Mass. (courtesy Historic New England)

A Celebrated Industry

123) Late eighteenth or early nineteenth century green glazed red earthenware jug attributed to Bristol County, Mass. (courtesy Historic New England)

A Celebrated Industry

124) Late eighteenth or early nineteenth century green glazed red earthenware jug attributed to Bristol County, Mass. (courtesy Winterthur)

125) Late eighteenth or early nineteenth century green glazed red earthenware jug attributed to Bristol County, Mass.; Lura Woodside Watkins Collection. (courtesy National Museum of American History at the Smithsonian Institute)

A Celebrated Industry

126) Late eighteenth or early nineteenth century green glazed red earthenware jug most likely made in Bristol County, Mass. (courtesy Lewis Scranton)

127) (Left) Late eighteenth or early nineteenth century green glazed red earthenware jug attributed to Bristol County, Mass.; Lura Woodside Watkins Collection (courtesy National Museum of American History at the Smithsonian Institute)

A Celebrated Industry

128) Late eighteenth or early nineteenth century green glazed red earthenware jug attributed to southeastern Massachusetts, Bristol County, Mass. or Cape Cod.

A Celebrated Industry

129) Late eighteenth or early nineteenth century red earthenware jug attributed to Bristol County, Mass. with modern tin handle. (courtesy Crocker Farm)

130) (Left) Late eighteenth or early nineteenth century red earthenware jug attributed to Bristol County, Mass. (courtesy Crocker Farm)

131) Late eighteenth or early nineteenth century green glazed red earthenware jug attributed to Bristol County, Mass. (courtesy Crocker Farm)

132) Late eighteenth or early nineteenth century red earthenware jug attributed to Bristol County, Mass.

A Celebrated Industry

133) Late eighteenth or early nineteenth century green glazed red earthenware pitcher and jug attributed to Bristol County, Mass. (courtesy Sam Herrup)

134) Late eighteenth or early nineteenth century red earthenware handled pot and jug attributed to Bristol County, Mass. (courtesy Lewis Scranton)

A Celebrated Industry

135) Late eighteenth or early nineteenth century green glazed red earthenware jug and pitcher attributed to Bristol County, Mass. (courtesy Lewis Scranton)

136) Late eighteenth or early nineteenth century green glazed red earthenware jug attributed to Bristol County, Mass. (courtesy Lewis Scranton)

A Celebrated Industry

137) Late eighteenth or early nineteenth century red earthenware jug attributed to Bristol County, Mass. (courtesy Skinner, Lewis Scranton Collection)

138) Late eighteenth or early nineteenth century red earthenware jug likely made in Bristol County, Mass. (courtesy Old Sturbridge Village)

A Celebrated Industry

139) Late eighteenth or early nineteenth century green glazed red earthenware jug attributed to Bristol County, Mass. (courtesy Winterthur)

A Celebrated Industry

140) Late eighteenth or early nineteenth century green glazed red earthenware jug attributed to Bristol County, Mass. (courtesy Winterthur)

A Celebrated Industry

141) Late eighteenth or early nineteenth century red earthenware jug attributed to Bristol County, Mass. (courtesy Winterthur)

A Celebrated Industry

142) (Right) Late eighteenth or early nineteenth century red earthenware jug attributed to Bristol County, Mass.; the other jug may have been made there as well. (courtesy Old Sturbridge Village)

A Celebrated Industry

143) Late eighteenth or early nineteenth century red earthenware jug attributed to Bristol County, Mass. (courtesy Old Sturbridge Village)

A Celebrated Industry

144a) Late eighteenth or early nineteenth century red earthenware jug attributed to Bristol County, Mass. The jug is also shown in picture 116.

144b) Similar glazed red earthenware jug from Bristol County, Mass. like that shown in picture 144a that was found by Chris Havey in Essex County, Mass.

A Celebrated Industry

145) Late eighteenth or early nineteenth century red earthenware pitcher attributed to Bristol County, Mass. (courtesy Northeast Auctions, previously owned by Charles D. Cook)

A Celebrated Industry

146) Late eighteenth or early nineteenth century red earthenware pitcher attributed to Bristol County, Mass. (courtesy Skinner & Jim and Janet Laverdiere)

147) Late eighteenth or early nineteenth century red earthenware handled pot probably made in southeastern Massachusetts or Bristol County. (courtesy Pook & Pook Inc.)

148) Late eighteenth or early nineteenth century green glazed red earthenware pitcher attributed to Bristol County, Mass. (courtesy Ron & Penny Dionne Collection and Antiques Associates at West Townsend)

A Celebrated Industry

149) Late eighteenth or early nineteenth century green glazed red earthenware handled pot attributed to Bristol County, Mass. (courtesy Winterthur)

150) Late eighteenth or early nineteenth century green glazed red earthenware pitcher attributed to Bristol County, Mass. (courtesy Skinner)

A Celebrated Industry

151) Late eighteenth or early nineteenth century green glazed red earthenware pitcher attributed to Bristol County, Mass. (courtesy Skinner, previously owned by Charles D. Cook)

A Celebrated Industry

152) Late eighteenth or early nineteenth century green glazed red earthenware pitcher attributed to Bristol County, Mass. (courtesy Winterthur)

A Celebrated Industry

153) Late eighteenth or early nineteenth century green glazed red earthenware pitcher attributed to Bristol County, Mass. (courtesy Ron & Penny Dionne Collection and Antiques Associates at West Townsend)

A Celebrated Industry

154) Late eighteenth or early nineteenth century red earthenware pitcher attributed to Bristol County, Mass. (courtesy Ron & Penny Dionne Collection and Antiques Associates at West Townsend)

155) Late eighteenth or early nineteenth century red earthenware pitcher attributed to Bristol County, Mass. (courtesy Ron & Penny Dionne Collection and Antiques Associates at West Townsend)

A Celebrated Industry

156) Late eighteenth or early nineteenth century green glazed red earthenware pitcher attributed to Bristol County, Mass. (courtesy Northeast Auctions and Dr. Mark Chaplin, previously owned by Lewis Scranton and illustrated in Slipped and Glazed: Regional American Redware)

A Celebrated Industry

157) Late eighteenth or early nineteenth century green glazed red earthenware pitcher attributed to Bristol County, Mass. (courtesy Northeast Auctions)

A Celebrated Industry

158) Late eighteenth or early nineteenth century red earthenware pitcher attributed to Bristol County, Mass. that was found in an estate in southern California (courtesy Loop Martinez)

159) Late eighteenth or early nineteenth century red earthenware pitcher attributed to Bristol County, Mass; this style of glaze and slip decoration is extremely rare today. (courtesy Pook & Pook Inc..)

A Celebrated Industry

160) Late eighteenth or early nineteenth century red earthenware pitcher attributed to Bristol County, Mass.

A Celebrated Industry

161a-161b) Late eighteenth or early nineteenth century green glazed red earthenware pitcher attributed to Bristol County, Mass. This pitcher was included in the first color plate published in The Magazine Antiques in December 1925. (courtesy The Bennington Museum and The Magazine Antiques)

A Celebrated Industry

162) Late eighteenth or early nineteenth century green glazed red earthenware pitcher attributed to Bristol County, Mass. (courtesy Old Sturbridge Village)

A Celebrated Industry

163) Late eighteenth or early nineteenth century green glazed red earthenware pitcher attributed to Bristol County, Mass.

A Celebrated Industry

164) Late eighteenth or early nineteenth century green glazed red earthenware pitcher attributed to Bristol County, Mass.

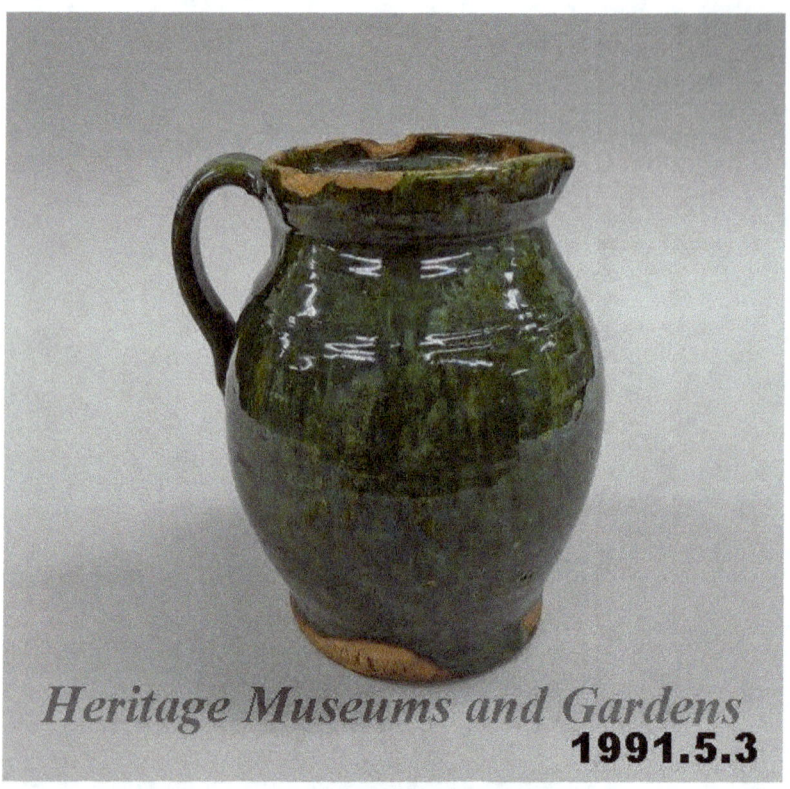

165) Late eighteenth or early nineteenth century green glazed red earthenware pitcher attributed to Bristol County, Mass. (courtesy Heritage Museums and Gardens)

A Celebrated Industry

166) Late eighteenth or early nineteenth century red earthenware pitcher attributed to Bristol County, Mass. (courtesy Skinner)

A Celebrated Industry

167) Late eighteenth or early nineteenth century green glazed red earthenware pitcher attributed to Bristol County, Mass. (courtesy Pook & Pook Inc.)

A Celebrated Industry

168) Late eighteenth or early nineteenth century red earthenware pitcher attributed to Bristol County, Mass.; Lura Woodside Watkins Collection. (courtesy National Museum of American History at the Smithsonian Institute)

169) Late eighteenth or early nineteenth century red earthenware pitcher likely made in Bristol County, Mass. (courtesy Lewis Scranton)

A Celebrated Industry

170) Late eighteenth or early nineteenth century red earthenware pitcher likely made in Bristol County, Mass. (courtesy Lewis Scranton)

A Celebrated Industry

171) Late eighteenth or early nineteenth century red earthenware pitcher likely made in Bristol County, Mass.

A Celebrated Industry

172) Late eighteenth or early nineteenth century red earthenware pitcher likely made in Bristol County, Mass.

A Celebrated Industry

173) Late eighteenth or early nineteenth century red earthenware pitcher likely made in Bristol County, Mass. (courtesy Historic Deerfield)

A Celebrated Industry

174) Late eighteenth or early nineteenth century red earthenware pitcher most likely made in Bristol County, Mass.

A Celebrated Industry

175) Late eighteenth or early nineteenth century red earthenware pitcher most likely made in Bristol County, Mass. (courtesy Historic Deerfield)

A Celebrated Industry

176) Eighteenth or early nineteenth century red earthenware pitcher most likely made in Bristol County, Mass. (courtesy Willis Henry & Jim and Janet Laverdiere)

A Celebrated Industry

177) Late eighteenth or early nineteenth century red earthenware pitcher most likely made in Bristol County, Mass. (courtesy Crocker Farm)

A Celebrated Industry

178) Late eighteenth or early nineteenth century red earthenware pitcher attributed to Bristol County, Mass.

A Celebrated Industry

179) Late eighteenth or early nineteenth century red earthenware pitcher attributed to Bristol County, Mass.

A Celebrated Industry

180) Late eighteenth or early nineteenth century red earthenware pitcher attributed to Bristol County, Mass., likely made by Somerset, Mass. based on archaeological evidence collected by Lura Woodside Watkins kept at the National Museum of American History at the Smithsonian Institute

A Celebrated Industry

181) Late eighteenth or early nineteenth century red earthenware pitcher attributed to Bristol County, Mass. (courtesy Historic New England)

182) Late eighteenth or early nineteenth century red earthenware handled pot attributed to Bristol County, Mass. (courtesy Skinner, Lewis Scranton Collection)

A Celebrated Industry

183) Late eighteenth or early nineteenth century red earthenware pitcher attributed to Bristol County, Mass. (courtesy Old Sturbridge Village)

A Celebrated Industry

184) Late eighteenth or early nineteenth century red earthenware pitcher likely made in Bristol County, Mass., shown to the right in the picture below. (courtesy Winterthur)

A Celebrated Industry

185) Late eighteenth or early nineteenth century red earthenware pitcher attributed to Bristol County, Mass. (Hilary and Paulette Nolan Collection)

A Celebrated Industry

186) Late eighteenth or early nineteenth century red earthenware pitcher attributed to Bristol County, Mass. (Skinner, previously owned by Charles D. Cook)

187) Late eighteenth or early nineteenth century red earthenware pitcher attributed to Bristol County, Mass. (courtesy Northeast Auctions)

A Celebrated Industry

188) Late eighteenth or early nineteenth century red earthenware pitchers attributed to Bristol County, Mass. (courtesy Old Sturbridge Village)

189) Late eighteenth or early nineteenth century red earthenware rundlet possibly made in Bristol County, Mass. (courtesy Northeast Auctions)

190) Late eighteenth or early nineteenth century red earthenware rundlet likely made in Bristol County, Mass. (courtesy Ron & Penny Dionne Collection and Antiques Associates at West Townsend)

A Celebrated Industry

191-192) Late eighteenth or early nineteenth century red earthenware rundlets possibly made in Bristol County, Mass. (courtesy Winterthur)

A Celebrated Industry

193) Late eighteenth or early nineteenth century red earthenware rundlet attributed to Bristol County, Mass. with slip decorated birds applied on each end. (courtesy Crocker Farm)

A Celebrated Industry

194) Late eighteenth or early nineteenth century green glazed red earthenware mug attributed to Bristol County, Mass. (courtesy Ron & Penny Dionne Collection and Antiques Associates at West Townsend)

A Celebrated Industry

195) Late eighteenth or early nineteenth century green glazed red earthenware mug attributed to Bristol County, Mass. (courtesy Ron & Penny Dionne Collection and Antiques Associates at West Townsend)

A Celebrated Industry

196) Late eighteenth or early nineteenth century green glazed red earthenware mug attributed to Bristol County, Mass. (courtesy Ron & Penny Dionne Collection and Antiques Associates at West Townsend)

A Celebrated Industry

197) Late eighteenth or early nineteenth century green glazed red earthenware mug attributed to Bristol County, Mass. (courtesy The Bennington Museum)

A Celebrated Industry

198) Late eighteenth or early nineteenth century green glazed red earthenware mug attributed to Bristol County, Mass.

A Celebrated Industry

199a) Late eighteenth or early nineteenth century red earthenware porringer attributed to Bristol County, Mass. (courtesy Winterthur)

199b) Similar form green glazed porringer painted for the Index of American Design by John Matulis (1910-2000) in 1936. (courtesy National Gallery of Art at the Smithsonian Institute)

A Celebrated Industry

200) Late eighteenth or early nineteenth century green glazed red earthenware bowl attributed to Bristol County, Mass.

A Celebrated Industry

201) Late eighteenth or early nineteenth century green glazed red earthenware bowl likely made in Bristol County, Mass., but may have also been made at the Upton Pottery in East Greenwich, R.I. (courtesy Winterthur)

A Celebrated Industry

202) Late eighteenth or early nineteenth century red earthenware bowls attributed to Bristol County, Mass. (courtesy Old Sturbridge Village)

203) Late eighteenth or early nineteenth century red earthenware bowl attributed to Bristol County, Mass. (courtesy Old Sturbridge Village)

A Celebrated Industry

204) Late eighteenth or early nineteenth century red earthenware shaving mug attributed to southeastern Massachusetts or Bristol County, Mass. (courtesy New Bedford Whaling Museum)

205) Late eighteenth or early nineteenth century green glazed red earthenware tea caddy likely made in Bristol County, Mass. (courtesy Larry Conklin)

A Celebrated Industry

206) Late eighteenth or early nineteenth century red earthenware inkwell attributed to Bristol County, Mass. (courtesy Crocker Farm, Hilary & Paulette Nolan Collection)

A Celebrated Industry

207) Eighteenth or early nineteenth century red earthenware teacup and saucer attributed to southeastern Massachusetts or Bristol County, Mass.; the teacup and saucer are shown to the right in the photo below. (courtesy Skinner and Lewis Scranton)

A Celebrated Industry

208) Late eighteenth or early nineteenth century green glazed red earthenware flask attributed to Bristol County, Mass. (courtesy Sam Herrup)

209) Late eighteenth or early nineteenth century slip decorated red earthenware bottle attributed to Bristol County, Mass. (courtesy Lewis Scranton)

210) Late eighteenth or early nineteenth century red earthenware flask possibly made in Bristol County, Mass. (courtesy Winterthur)

A Celebrated Industry

211) Late eighteenth or early nineteenth century red earthenware harvest jug attributed to Bristol County, Mass. (courtesy Skinner, formerly owned by Charles D. Cook)

A Celebrated Industry

212) Late eighteenth or early nineteenth century red earthenware harvest jug attributed to Bristol County, Mass. (courtesy Winterthur)

213) Late eighteenth or early nineteenth century red earthenware harvest jug attributed to Bristol County, Mass. (courtesy Sam Herrup)

A Celebrated Industry

214) Late eighteenth or early nineteenth century red earthenware harvest jug attributed to Bristol County, Mass. (courtesy Winterthur)

A Celebrated Industry

215) Late eighteenth or early nineteenth century red earthenware harvest jug attributed to Bristol County, Mass. (courtesy Winterthur)

216) Late eighteenth or early nineteenth century red earthenware harvest jug attributed to Bristol County, Mass. Found years ago by Paul DeCoste in Rowley, Mass., and later sold in the Nolan Collection at Northeast Auctions. (courtesy Paul DeCoste)

A Celebrated Industry

217) Early nineteenth century red earthenware oil lamp likely made in Bristol County, Mass. Form is most likely related to the jars illustrated in pictures 76-78.

A Celebrated Industry

218) Early nineteenth century red earthenware oil lamp likely made in Bristol County, Mass. (courtesy Chris & Bernadette Evans)

A Celebrated Industry

219) Late eighteenth or early nineteenth century red earthenware barrel probably made in Bristol County, Mass., form is similar to the rundlets manufactured in Bristol County.

220) Late eighteenth or early nineteenth century red earthenware flask in the form of a ball possibly made in Bristol County, Mass. (courtesy Historic New England)

A Celebrated Industry

221) Late eighteenth or early nineteenth century slip decorated red earthenware pan attributed to Bristol County, Mass. (courtesy Flying Pig Antiques)

222) Late eighteenth or early nineteenth century slip decorated red earthenware pan attributed to Bristol County, Mass. (courtesy Historic New England)

A Celebrated Industry

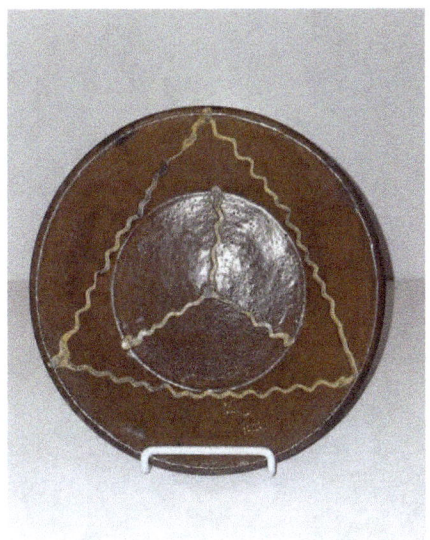

223) Late eighteenth or early nineteenth century slip decorated red earthenware pan attributed to Bristol County, Mass.

224) Late eighteenth or early nineteenth century slip decorated red earthenware pan attributed to Bristol County, Mass. (courtesy Little Compton, Rhode Island Historical Society)

A Celebrated Industry

225) Late eighteenth or early nineteenth century slip decorated red earthenware pan attributed to Bristol County, Mass. (courtesy Sam Herrup)

226) Late eighteenth or early nineteenth century green glazed red earthenware bowl possibly made in southeastern Massachusetts or Bristol County, Mass. (courtesy Larry Conklin)

A Celebrated Industry

227) Late eighteenth or early nineteenth century slip decorated red earthenware pans attributed to Bristol County, Mass. (courtesy Old Sturbridge Village, previously owned by Roger Bacon)

A Celebrated Industry

228) Late eighteenth or early nineteenth century green glazed red earthenware pitcher attributed to Bristol County, Mass. (courtesy Private Collection, previously owned by Ron & Penny Dionne)

229) Late eighteenth or early nineteenth century green glazed red earthenware pitcher attributed to Bristol County, Mass. (courtesy Private Collection)

A Celebrated Industry

230-234 All late eighteenth or early nineteenth century Bristol County, Mass. Jar pictured to the left in the middle row was formerly a part of the Huntington Collection that sold in Maine in 1974. (courtesy Vince Martonis)

A Celebrated Industry

235) Late eighteenth or early nineteenth century green glazed red earthenware jug attributed to Bristol County, Mass. (courtesy Private Collection)

236) Late eighteenth or early nineteenth century red earthenware jug attributed to Bristol County, Mass. (courtesy Private Collection)

A Celebrated Industry

237-241) All late eighteenth or early nineteenth century Bristol County, Mass., although the green glazed flowerpot may have been produced elsewhere in southeastern Massachusetts or on Cape Cod. (courtesy Brian Bartizek)

A Celebrated Industry

242) Late eighteenth or early nineteenth century red earthenware jars attributed to Bristol County, Mass. (courtesy Sam Herrup)

243) Late eighteenth or early nineteenth century red earthenware jar attributed to Bristol County, Mass. (courtesy Sam Herrup)

A Celebrated Industry

244) Late eighteenth or early nineteenth century green glazed red earthenware pitcher attributed to Bristol County, Mass. (courtesy Sam Herrup)

A Celebrated Industry

245) Late eighteenth or early nineteenth century green glazed red earthenware jar attributed to Bristol County, Mass. (courtesy Sam Herrup)

246) Late eighteenth or early nineteenth century red earthenware jug attributed to Bristol County, Mass. (courtesy Sam Herrup)

A Celebrated Industry

247) Late eighteenth or early nineteenth century red earthenware jug attributed to Bristol County, Mass. (courtesy Sam Herrup)

A Celebrated Industry

248-250) All late eighteenth or early nineteenth century attributed to Bristol County, Mass. (courtesy Sam Herrup)

A Celebrated Industry

251) Large late eighteenth or early nineteenth century red earthenware jug attributed to Bristol County, Mass. (courtesy Sam Herrup)

A Celebrated Industry

252) Late eighteenth or early nineteenth century red earthenware handled pot attributed to Bristol County, Mass. (courtesy Dr. Mark Chaplin and AAAWT)

253) Late eighteenth or early nineteenth century red earthenware jug attributed to Bristol County, Mass. (courtesy Crocker Farm)

254) Late eighteenth or early nineteenth century red earthenware jug attributed to Bristol County, Mass. (courtesy Crocker Farm)

A Celebrated Industry

255-262) All late eighteenth or early nineteenth century Bristol County, Mass., bottom left was previously owned by Charles D. Cook. (courtesy Skinner)

A Celebrated Industry

263-266) All probably or likely eighteenth or early nineteenth century southeastern Massachusetts or Bristol County, Mass. (courtesy Skinner)

267-268) All late eighteenth or early nineteenth century and attributed to Bristol County, Mass. except the jar shown to the far left in picture 267. (courtesy Skinner).

A Celebrated Industry

269) Late eighteenth or early nineteenth century red earthenware flask in the form of a ball possibly made in Bristol County, Mass. (courtesy Willis Henry)

270-273) All late eighteenth or early nineteenth century and attributed to Bristol County, Mass. (courtesy Willis Henry)

A Celebrated Industry

274) Late eighteenth or early nineteenth century red earthenware jar attributed to Bristol County, Mass., inscribed on the base with the letter "D." (courtesy Brian Cullity)

A Celebrated Industry

275) Late eighteenth or early nineteenth century red earthenware jar attributed to Bristol County, Mass. that was previously found in Minnesota. (Crocker Farm)

276) Late eighteenth or early nineteenth century red earthenware jar likely made in Bristol County, Mass. (courtesy Sam Herrup)

A Celebrated Industry

277) Late eighteenth or early nineteenth century red earthenware jug attributed to Bristol County, Mass. (courtesy Dr. Mark Chaplin)

278) Late eighteenth or early nineteenth century red earthenware jar attributed to Bristol County, Mass. (courtesy Historic New England)

A Celebrated Industry

279) Late eighteenth or early nineteenth century red earthenware jar attributed to Bristol County, Mass. Although, this jar was previously published as being from the Nathaniel Seymour (1763-1849) Pottery in West Hartford, CT in Figure 43 in Early New England Potters and Their Wares, likely as a result of an old tag adhered to the base of the jar, reading, "Seymour Pottery Hartford Conn." (courtesy Historic New England)

A Celebrated Industry

280) Late eighteenth or early nineteenth century red earthenware jar possibly made in Bristol County, Mass. (courtesy Ron & Penny Dionne Collection and Antiques Associates at West Townsend)

A Celebrated Industry

281) Late eighteenth or early nineteenth century red earthenware shaving cup attributed to southeastern Mass. This was previously owned by Hilary & Paulette Nolan.

282) The eighteenth century slip decorated mug shown to the left was published in picture 28 in Early England Potters and Their Wares and thought to have possibly been made in southeastern Mass. about 1750. It may have actually been made in Charlestown, Mass. around the same period. (courtesy National Museum of American History at the Smithsonian Institute)

A Celebrated Industry

283) Late eighteenth or early nineteenth century red earthenware pitchers likely both manufactured in southeastern Massachusetts. (courtesy Dr. Mark Chaplin)

284) Late eighteenth or early nineteenth century red earthenware jar attributed to Bristol County, Mass. A number of these type of jar were converted into lamp bases in the twentieth century. (courtesy Private Massachusetts Collection)

285) The late eighteenth or early nineteenth century red earthenware jar shown to the left is attributed to Bristol County, Mass. (courtesy Private Massachusetts Collection)

A Celebrated Industry

286-287) Late eighteenth or early nineteenth century slip decorated red earthenware dish and jar attributed to Bristol County, Mass. This dish is also illustrated in picture number 225. (courtesy Bill Taylor)

288) Late eighteenth or early nineteenth century red earthenware jar attributed to Bristol County, Mass. that was found in Rhode Island. (courtesy Bill Taylor)

289) Late eighteenth or early nineteenth century red earthenware jar attributed to Bristol County, Mass. that was found in Indian Hill, West Tisbury on Martha's Vineyard and likely also retaining a history of ownership on the island. (courtesy Bill Taylor)

A Celebrated Industry

290) Late eighteenth or early nineteenth century red earthenware rundlet possibly manufactured in Bristol County, Mass. (courtesy Yale University Art Gallery)

291) Jar shown to the right is a late eighteenth or early nineteenth century green glazed red earthenware jar attributed to Bristol County, Mass. (courtesy Bidwell House Museum)

292-293) Late eighteenth or early nineteenth century green glazed red earthenware jug and jar attributed to Bristol County, Mass. (courtesy Litchfield, Connecticut Historical Society)

A Celebrated Industry

294) Late eighteenth or early nineteenth century green glazed red earthenware jar attributed to southeastern Mass., possibly made in Bristol County. (courtesy Private Collection)

A Celebrated Industry

295) Late eighteenth or early nineteenth century green glazed red earthenware jar attributed to Bristol County, Mass. The jar is also decorated with bands of straight and wavy incised lines along the rim and body of the jar. (courtesy Jim Mahoney)

A Celebrated Industry

296) Late eighteenth or early nineteenth century red earthenware jar attributed to Bristol County, Mass. (courtesy Jim Mahoney)

297) Late eighteenth or early nineteenth century red earthenware jug attributed to Bristol County, Mass. (courtesy Jim Mahoney)

A Celebrated Industry

298) Late eighteenth or early nineteenth century red earthenware jar attributed to Bristol County, Mass. (courtesy Historic Deerfield)

A Celebrated Industry

299) Late eighteenth or early nineteenth century green glazed red earthenware jar attributed to southeastern Massachusetts, possibly manufactured in Bristol County. See Figure 5.33 for more information. (courtesy Historic Deerfield)

A Celebrated Industry

300) Late eighteenth or early nineteenth century green glazed red earthenware jug attributed to southeastern Mass. or Bristol County, Mass. (courtesy Historic Deerfield)

View of the handle. (courtesy Historic Deerfield)

A Celebrated Industry

301) Late eighteenth or early nineteenth century green glazed red earthenware jar likely made in Bristol County, Mass. The jar is also decorated with combed incised decoration. (courtesy Historic Deerfield)

A Celebrated Industry

302) (Left) Possibly an eighteenth century creamer or small pitcher made by John Henry Benner in Abington, Mass., otherwise likely another Massachusetts potter. (courtesy Christies)

303) Grouping of Bristol County, Mass. red earthenware some of which is pictured individually elsewhere in this book. (courtesy Sam Herrup)

A Celebrated Industry

304) Late eighteenth or early nineteenth century green glazed red earthenware mug with black spots attributed to southeastern Mass. or Bristol County, Mass. (courtesy Historic Deerfield)

A Celebrated Industry

305) Late eighteenth or early nineteenth century red earthenware pitcher attributed to Bristol County, Mass. (courtesy Historic Deerfield)

A Celebrated Industry

306) Late eighteenth or early nineteenth century green glazed red earthenware jar attributed to Bristol County, Mass.; previously owned by Charles D. Cook. (courtesy New Haven Auctions)

307) (Left) Coastal Mass. red earthenware jug, circa early 1800s; (Right) Red earthenware jug possibly made in Southeastern Mass. (courtesy New Haven Auctions)

A Celebrated Industry

308) Late eighteenth or early nineteenth century green glazed red earthenware pitcher attributed to Bristol County, Mass. (courtesy Historic Deerfield)

A Celebrated Industry

309) Late eighteenth or early nineteenth century green glazed red earthenware jar attributed to Bristol County, Mass. (courtesy Historic Deerfield)

A Celebrated Industry

310) Late eighteenth or early nineteenth century red earthenware jar attributed to Bristol County, Mass. inscribed on the side with the number "111" or three slash marks that likely matched a lid with the same inscription. (courtesy Historic Deerfield)

A Celebrated Industry

311a) Late eighteenth or early nineteenth century slip decorated red earthenware dish attributed to Bristol County, Mass. (courtesy Winterthur)

311b) Eighteenth or early nineteenth century slip decorated red earthenware dish attributed to southeastern Massachusetts.

A Celebrated Industry

312) Late eighteenth or early nineteenth century slip decorated red earthenware dish attributed to Bristol County, Mass. (courtesy Hollis Brodrick)

313) Small early nineteenth century New England red earthenware pot retaining its original lid. Both the lid and the pot are incised with the Roman numeral "VIII." This type of numbering system was applied by both the Bradfords and in Bristol County, Mass. (courtesy Albert Hastings Pitkin Collection at the Wadsworth Atheneum)

314) Late eighteenth or early nineteenth century red earthenware jar attributed to Bristol County, Mass. (courtesy Historic Deerfield)

A Celebrated Industry

315) Large late eighteenth or early nineteenth century red earthenware pitcher attributed to Bristol County, Mass. (courtesy Jim and Janet Laverdiere)

A Celebrated Industry

316) Late eighteenth or early nineteenth century red earthenware jar attributed to Bristol County, Mass. (courtesy Jim and Janet Laverdiere)

A Celebrated Industry

317) Probably eighteenth century green glazed red earthenware teacup thought to have been made at the Upton Pottery in East Greenwich, R.I. It was published with this attribution in an article written by Charles D. Cook for the January 1931 issue of The Magazine Antiques, titled, Early Rhode Island Pottery, although the glaze also closely resembles a style recovered by Lura Woodside Watkins in Somerset, Bristol County, Mass. now at the Smithsonian Institute in Washington, D.C.; see Chapter 5, Figure 5.21. (courtesy Jim and Janet Laverdiere) Also see the Introduction to this book for more information.

A Celebrated Industry

318-319) Late eighteenth or early nineteenth century red earthenware jar and three jugs attributed to Bristol County, Mass., some of the jugs are also pictured elsewhere in this book. (courtesy Jim and Janet Laverdiere)

A Celebrated Industry

320) Late eighteenth or early nineteenth century red earthenware jar attributed to Bristol County, Mass., also illustrated elsewhere in this book. (courtesy Jim and Janet Laverdiere)

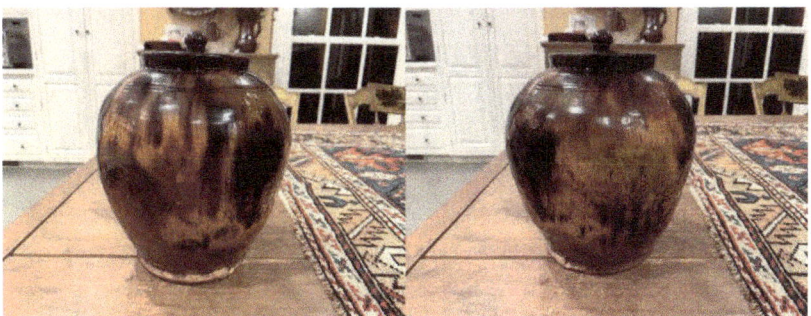

A Celebrated Industry

321) Late eighteenth or early nineteenth century green glazed red earthenware pitcher attributed to Bristol County, Mass. (courtesy Jim and Janet Laverdiere)

A Celebrated Industry

322) Late eighteenth or early nineteenth century jar attributed to Bristol County, Mass. with an inscribed letter "V" on the base; the original lid would have been inscribed with the same letter. (courtesy Historic Deerfield)

323) Small eighteenth or early nineteenth century red earthenware jug likely made in either southeastern Mass. or Bristol County, Mass. (courtesy Historic Deerfield)

A Celebrated Industry

324) Early nineteenth century red earthenware jar possibly made in southern Massachusetts. The base of the jar and the lid are both inscribed with the number "7." (courtesy Historic Deerfield)

A Celebrated Industry

325) Early nineteenth century pitcher that is similar to wares manufactured in southeastern Mass., Bristol County and by the Clark family in Lyndeborough, N.H. (courtesy Historic Deerfield)

326) Late eighteenth or early nineteenth century jar and jug attributed to Bristol County, Mass., also pictured elsewhere in this book. (courtesy Sam Herrup)

A Celebrated Industry

327-328) (left to right) Late eighteenth or early nineteenth century red earthenware jug, jar, handled pot and pitcher all attributed to Bristol County, Mass., except the jug to the far left, which may be from southeastern Mass. or another location, and the pitcher to the far right could also be related to Peter Clark. (courtesy Roger Pheulpin)

329) Late eighteenth or early nineteenth century red earthenware jar attributed to Bristol County, Mass. (courtesy Connecticut Historical Society and Historic New England)

A Celebrated Industry

330) Late eighteenth or early nineteenth century green glazed red earthenware jug attributed to Bristol County, Mass. (courtesy Historic Deerfield)

331) Late eighteenth or early nineteenth century red earthenware bowl possibly from Bristol County, Mass. and perhaps related to the jar from Nina Fletcher Little's Collection at Historic New England illustrated in picture 279. (courtesy Crocker Farm, November 3, 2007)

A Celebrated Industry

332-333) Late eighteenth or early nineteenth century red earthenware jars attributed to Bristol County, Mass. Due to the size and shape of some of these jars, a number of them were converted into lamps in the 1900s. (courtesy Nadeau's Auction Gallery Inc.)

A Celebrated Industry

334-335) Late eighteenth or early nineteenth century red earthenware jars and jug attributed to Bristol County, Mass. (courtesy James Julia, Pook & Pook and the Cobbs)

A Celebrated Industry

336-337) Late eighteenth or early nineteenth century red earthenware jugs possibly manufactured in southeastern Mass. or Bristol County, otherwise elsewhere in coastal Mass. (courtesy Warner House Museum in Portsmouth, N.H. and the Little Compton, R.I. Historical Society)

A Celebrated Industry

338) Late eighteenth or early nineteenth century red earthenware jar attributed to Bristol County, Mass; from David Good's collection. (courtesy New Haven Auctions)

339) Early nineteenth century red earthenware jar possibly manufactured at the Bradford Pottery in Kingston, Mass. Also illustrated elsewhere in this book. (courtesy New Haven Auctions)

340-341) Late eighteenth or early nineteenth century green glazed red earthenware jar and jug attributed to Bristol County, Mass.; from David Good's collection. (courtesy New Haven Auctions)

A Celebrated Industry

342-343) Late eighteenth or early nineteenth century red earthenware pitcher and jar attributed to Bristol County, Mass. (courtesy John McInnis)

344) Far right is a late eighteenth or early nineteenth century green glazed red earthenware jar attributed to southeastern Massachusetts. (courtesy Sam Herrup)

A Celebrated Industry

345) Late eighteenth or early nineteenth century red earthenware jar attributed to Bristol County, Mass. (courtesy AAAWT, Hilary & Paulette Nolan Collection)

346) Eighteenth or early nineteenth century red earthenware handled pot probably made along coastal Massachusetts, and very possibly from southeastern Massachusetts. (courtesy Pook & Pook)

A Celebrated Industry

347) Late eighteenth or early nineteenth century red earthenware jug attributed to Bristol County, Mass. (courtesy Webb-Deane-Stevens Museum in Wethersfield, Connecticut)

A Celebrated Industry

348) Late eighteenth or early nineteenth century green glazed red earthenware pitcher attributed to Bristol County, Mass. (courtesy Sam Forsythe)

A Celebrated Industry

349) Late eighteenth or early nineteenth century red earthenware jar attributed to Bristol County, Mass. The base is inscribed with probably a zero. A slash is usually drawn through a zero to distinguish it from the letter "O." (courtesy Brian Cullity)

A Celebrated Industry

350) Early nineteenth century red earthenware jar that is related to the jars illustrated in Chapter 4 The Archaeology of the Kingston Pottery. There are very few jars known to exist like this today. (courtesy Tim Gould)

A Celebrated Industry

351) Late eighteenth or early nineteenth century red earthenware pitcher attributed to Bristol County, Mass. The pitcher is manufactured with the typical Bristol County footed base and handle.

A Celebrated Industry

352) Late eighteenth or early nineteenth century red earthenware jar attributed to Bristol County, Mass. Some of the orange glaze has turned a pinkish or peach color, a rare glaze color to find from Bristol County today. The jar is also inscribed with four slash marks.

A Celebrated Industry

353) Probably an eighteenth century red earthenware cup adorned with some slip decoration. The form of the cup is similar to styles produced in Charlestown, Massachusetts before 1775, as well as in Essex County, Mass. in the 1700s, although the glaze colors are also reminiscent to some produced by John Henry Benner in Abington, Mass.

354) Late eighteenth century red earthenware pitcher made in either southeastern Mass. or Bristol County, Mass. (courtesy Hindman Auctions)

A Celebrated Industry

> List of Some of the Potters Employed in Southeastern Massachusetts, Bristol County and Cape Cod

The area in green is where these potters worked in southeastern Massachusetts, Bristol County and Cape Cod, where much of the production took place around the Taunton River near New Bedford.

Applegate, Asher
1850, 1860
Taunton

Benner, John Henry
1755-1795
Quincy (Germantown), Abington

Boyce, Enoch
1814-1876
Berkley

Boyce, Enoch
1773-1859
Berkley

Boyce, John
1817-1893
Berkley

Boyce, John Sr.
Ca. 1760-1839
Berkley

Boyce, William
1727/28-1799
Berkley, Salem

Bradford, Noah
1761-1841
Barnstable, Kingston

Bradford, Stephen
1771-1837
Kingston

Bradford, Stephen Jr.
1807
Kingston

Brown, George
Somerset

Chace, Asa
1744-1812
Somerset

Chace, Benjamin Cartwright
Somerset

Chace, Benjamin G.
1812
Somerset

Chace, Clark
1780-1836
Somerset

Chace, Clark
1814-1881
Somerset

Chace, Elijiah Cornell
1771-1812
Somerset

Chace, Enoch Boyce
1794-1825
Somerset

Chace, Joseph
1785-1815
Somerset

Chace, Leonard
Somerset

Chace, Lloyd
Somerset

Chace, Marcus
Taunton

Chace, Stephen
Ca. 1769-1815
Somerset

Chace, Stephen II
Died Ca. 1824
Somerset

Chace, Stephen III
Died Ca. 1843
Somerset

Clark, Peter I
1743-1826
Braintree and Lyndeborough, N.H.

Cleveland, Benjamin
1856
Somerset

Collins, Samuel B.
Somerset

Cornell, Elijiah
1771-1862
Somerset, New York State and Albion, Mich.

Cranch, Richard
1753-?
Braintree (Dorchester)

Dalton, R.C.
1866
Taunton

Dunbar, Peter
Born July 8, 1822
Taunton

Faxon, Ebenezer
1749-1811
Braintree and West Hartford

Gray, Joseph
1854
Somerset

Hathaway, Charles F.
1880, 1895
Somerset

Kenney, Thomas
Somerset

Letts, Alfred W.
1857
Taunton

Levins, Thomas
1850
Taunton

Neil, Jonathan
Ca. 1730
Scituate

Osborn, Paul
1740, 1760
Berkley and South Danvers

Parker, Benjamin
1849
West Barnstable

Daniel Parker
1831
West Barnstable

Palmer, Joseph
1753
Braintree

Purinton, Clark
1730-1786
Somerset

Purinton, Clark Jr.
Died 1817
Somerset

Purinton, Daniel
d. May 23, 1764
South Danvers

Purinton, David
1856
Somerset

Purinton, Dexter
1856
Somerset

Purinton, George
1835
Somerset

Purington, David
1856
Somerset

Purington, Dexter H.
1856
Somerset

Purington, George S.
1856
Somerset

Purington, Samuel S.
1856
Somerset

Seaver, William
1743/44-1815
Taunton

Seaver, John
Born March 26, 1779
Taunton

Shove, Asa
1741-1826
Berkley

Shove, Azariah
1749-1814
Berkley

Shove, Edward
1716-1778
Berkley

Shove, George
1738-1793
Berkley

Shove, Nathaniel
1723-1774
Swansea

Shove, Samuel
1740-1764
Berkley

Shove, Theophilus
1741-1803
Somerset

Standish, Alexander
Born October 28, 1809
Taunton

Synan, Patrick
1893
Somerset

Synan, William
1893
Somerset

Upton, Isaac
Born. October 6, 1736
Berkley and East Greenwich, R.I.

Upton, Samuel
Born April 3, 1748
Berkley and East Greenwich, R.I.

Wright, Franklin T.
1849, 1867
Taunton

Wyman, George E.
1866
Taunton

> Bibliography

A Most Important Auction. Early Americana The Private Collection Formed by the Late Oliver E. Williams. Rockport, Mass: Richard W. Worthington, Inc., 1968.

Beranek, Christa M., Kathryn A. Catlin, Katharine M. Johnson & Laura W. Ng, *Documentary Research and Archaeological Investigations at the Waite-Kirby-Potter Site, Westport, Massachusetts.* University of Massachusetts at Boston, Andrew Fiske Memorial Center for Archaeological Research Publications, 2010

Bihler and Coger Advertisement. *The Magazine Antiques Antiques*, January 1974

Brown III, Marley R. & Steven R. Pendery. "Plymouth, Massachusetts." *Ceramics in America,* 2017.

Chartier, Craig. *Report on the C-21/Allerton/Prence/Cushman Site, Kingston, Massachusetts.* Plymouth Archaeological Rediscovery Project, 2015.

_____. *Report on the 2017 Excavations at the Sturgis Library Barnstable, MA*. Plymouth Archaeological Rediscovery Project, 2018.

_____. *A Brief Report on the William Bradford II Site (Colonial 6/ C-06) Kingston, Massachusetts.* Plymouth Archaeological Rediscovery Project, 2019.

Cherry, Caroline L., Charles L. Cherry & John W. Oliver Jr. *Founded by Friends: The Quaker Heritage of 15 American Colleges and Universities.* Lanham, MD: Scarecrow Press, Inc., 2007.

Cook, Charles D. "Early Rhode Island Pottery." *The Magazine Antiques*, January 1931.

Cornell, John. *Genealogy of the Cornell Family.* New York: Press of T.A. Wright, 1902.

Cullity, Brian. *Slipped and Glazed: Regional American Redware.* Sandwich, Mass.: Heritage Plantation of Sandwich, 1991, 28.

Deetz, James & Derek Wheeler. *Report on the Excavations at the Joseph Howland Homesite.* Plymouth Archaeological Rediscovery Project, 2017.

Deyo, Simeon L. *History of Barnstable County, Massachusetts 1620-1637-1686-1890.* New York: Blake, 1890.

Dorf, Philip. *The Builder: A Biography of Ezra Cornell.* New York: The MacMillan Company, 1952.

Early American Country Antiques at Public Auction: The Exclusive Property of Mr. and Mrs. Christopher Huntington. Harrison, ME: Morrill's Auction, Inc., 1974.

Galvin, William Francis. *Historic & Archaeological Resources of Cape Cod & the Islands.* The Massachusetts Historical Commission, 1986.

Greene, Daniel Howland. *History of the Town of East Greenwich and Adjacent Territory From 1677 to 1877.* Providence: J.A. & R.A., Printers and Publishers, 1877.

Hurd, Duane Hamilton. *History of Bristol County, Massachusetts, with biographical sketches of many of its pioneers and prominent men.* Philadelphia: J.W. Lewis & Co., 1883.

Jobe, Brock, Jack O'Brien and Gary R. Sullivan. *Harbor and Home: Furniture of Southeastern Massachusetts, 1710-1850.* Lebanon, NH: The University Press of New England, 2009: 27-29.

Lang, Susan. "The Ezra Files: A family ever on the move." *Cornell Chronicle*, January 24, 2007.

Loan Exhibition of Early American Furniture and Decorative Arts (Boston), December 8-29, 1925, 50.

National Parks Service, 2017. African Meeting House, Retrieve. https://www.nps.gov/boaf/learn/historyculture/amh.htm.

New England Redware Collection of Paulette and Hilary Nolan. Manchester, N.H.: Northeast Auctions, 2004.

Preserve Peirce Account Book, 1757-1766. Wilmington, DE: Winterthur Library Collection.

Ramsay, John. "Early American Pottery: A Resume." *The Magazine Antiques*, October 1931.

Spargo, John. *Early American Pottery and China.* New York: Garden City Publishing, 1926, Plate 2.

Sulya, Martha L. Ubiquitous and Unfamiliar: Earthenware Pottery Production Techniques and the Bradford Family Pottery of Kingston, MA. UMass Boston: Masters Thesis, 2015.

Thomas, Justin. "Carl Mehwaldt: A Pioneer German-American Potter And 19th-Century Immigrant." *Antiques & Auction News,* October 8, 2021.

_____. *The Dawn of Independence, the Death of an Industry: The Pottery of Charlestown, Massachusetts.* Beverly, Mass.: Historic Beverly, 2020.

_____. "A Charlestown Sugar Bowl: The Rediscovery of a Redware Masterpiece." *New England Antiques Journal*, February 2016.

_____. "A Pioneering Potter: Samuel Marshall of Portsmouth, New Hampshire." *New England Antiques Journal*, April 2017.

_____. "The Pottery Industry in Southeastern Massachusetts." *Maine Antique Digest,* June 2017.

_____. "Digging Into the Peabody Potteries." *New England Antiques Journal*, November 2017.

_____. "The Red Earthenware Manufactured in River Edge, New Jersey." *Antiques & Auction News,* January 8, 2021.

_____. "The Upton Pottery in East Greenwich." *East Greenwich Historic Preservation Society Newsletter*, May 2019.

_____. "The Red Earthenware Industry in Concord, New Hampshire." *Maine Antique Digest*, June 2021.

_____. "A Look At 19th-Century Red Earthenware Figures Made in Pennsylvania." *Antiques & Auction News*, August 28, 2020.

Trayser, Donald G. *Barnstable: Three Centuries of a Cape Cod Town.* Hyannis, Mass.: F.B. & F.P. Goss, 1939.

Watkins, Lura Woodside. *Early New England Potters and Their Wares.* Cambridge, Mass.: Harvard University Press, 1950, 46-47.

ABOUT THE AUTHOR

Justin W. Thomas is a collector and researcher into the history of American utilitarian pottery production from the seventeenth through the twentieth century. He has authored a number of research articles for various regional and national publications, guest curated a major exhibit at the Custom House Maritime Museum in Newburyport, Mass. about the local eighteenth, nineteenth and early twentieth century potters, as well as helped author the exhibit catalog, *Potters on the Merrimac: A Century of New England* Ceramics, and authored the books, *The Beverly Pottery: The Wares of Charles A. Lawrence, The Moses B. Paige Company: The Last of the Peabody Potteries, The Dawn of Independence, the Death of an Industry: The Pottery of Charlestown, Massachusetts* and *South Amesbury's Red Earthenware & Stoneware: The 1791-1820 William Pecker Pottery*.

About Historic Beverly

The mission of Historic Beverly is to share Beverly's history with everyone through our 3 houses, 5 centuries, and 1000s of stories: by collecting and preserving Beverly's history; inspiring the community to engage with history; and making history accessible to all. For more information on our collections, properties, programming or publications, please visit or contact us at 978.922.1186 or info@historicbeverly.net.

About Historic Deerfield

Historic Deerfield is a museum dedicated to the heritage and preservation of Deerfield, Massachusetts, and the history of the Connecticut River Valley. Its historic houses, museums and programs provide visitors with an understanding of New England's historic villages and countryside. For more information, visit or call 413.775.7214.

About the National Museum of American History

The National Museum of American History collects, preserves and displays the heritage of the United States in the areas of social, political, cultural, scientific and military history. Among the items on display is the original Star-Spangled banner. The museum is part of the Smithsonian Institute and located on the National Mall at 14th Street and Constitution Avenue NW in Washington, D.C. For more information, visit or call 202.633-1000.

About Plimouth Plantation

Plimouth Plantation is a living history museum in Plymouth, Massachusetts, founded in 1947. It attempts to replicate the original settlement of the Plymouth Colony established in the seventeenth century by the English colonists who became known as pilgrims. For more information, visit or call 508.746.1622.

www.ingramcontent.com/pod-product-compliance
Lightning Source LLC
Chambersburg PA
CBHW050322020526
44117CB00031B/1437